Understanding The Baptist Faith & Message
A Simple Study for Southern Baptists

Rob Phillips

**high
street
press**

Acknowledgements:

Executive editor: Dr. John Yeats
Senior Editor: Gary Ledbetter
Cover design and graphics: Katie Shull
Layout: Brianna Boes, Tony Boes
Production management: Gary Ledbetter
Electronic production: Brianna Boes
Scripture verification: Christie Dowell
Proofreading: Christie Dowell, Nancy Phillips

High Street Press is the publishing arm of the Missouri Baptist Convention (MBC) and exists because of the generous support of Missouri Baptists through the Cooperative Program. To learn more about the MBC and the way nearly 1,800 affiliated churches cooperate voluntarily for the sake of the gospel, visit mobaptist.org. To learn more about High Street Press, visit highstreet.press.

Contents

Foreword

Always be ready to give a defense to anyone who asks you for a
reason for the hope that is in you.

— *1 Peter 3:15*

With the above directive in mind, the 1999 Southern Baptist
Convention voted for then-president Paige Patterson to appoint a
committee to review *The Baptist Faith & Message* and bring any
recommendations for revisions to the next annual meeting. Facing the
challenges of a new century, messengers to the convention voted
overwhelmingly for a reexamination of our confessional statement. It
was clear that in a culture that had become hostile to the idea of absolute
truth, this generation of Southern Baptists must set forth and clarify the
veracity of Scripture as they understood it. This was especially true in
light of the Conservative Resurgence (1979 - 1995) and the need to
address issues that had arisen since the adoption of the 1963 *Baptist
Faith & Message.* Just as the 1963 Convention saw the need to address a
document that was thirty-eight years old, so the 2000 Convention did as
it approached its own thirty-eighth year.

Given this charge, *The Baptist Faith & Message* 2000 study
committee was formed. It was my privilege to be a part of this committee

and to be present for all of the meetings. The committee Dr. Patterson appointed was representative of Southern Baptist life. It was diverse, not only in gender, but also in ethnicity, representing the African American, Hispanic, and Asian communities. It included theologians, pastors, a Baptist Student Union director, a state convention's Woman's Missionary Union and Women's Ministry director, seminary presidents, an agency head, and laypersons. Only persons committed to the inerrancy of Scripture were appointed to the committee.

The chair of the committee was the gracious and irreplaceable Adrian Rogers, who conducted each meeting with efficiency, humility, and humor. At the first meeting, Dr. Rogers challenged the committee to consider the various questions that had arisen regarding the 1963 version of *The Baptist Faith & Message*. We were then encouraged to discuss and examine carefully each issue raised by these questions and its relation to Baptist beliefs. Dr. Rogers was quite firm that there be no discrepancy or ambiguity in our language, since words communicate the essence of our faith. We also wanted to retain as much language from the 1925 and 1963 versions as possible.

There were several pressing doctrinal questions that the committee felt must be clarified. For example, we felt it was important to address a current theological trend called "The Openness of God," which challenged the concept of the omniscience and foreknowledge of God. This was addressed in Article II, "God." Another controversy at the time was the promotion of women in the pastorate by some Baptists. Article VI, "The Church," identified the scriptural basis for the office of pastor. As women on the committee, Heather King Moore and I believed, along with the other committee members, this was an important issue within Baptist life and the broader culture of evangelicalism. Due to the Conservative Resurgence, the committee felt it must address the inspiration and authority of Scripture. Article I, "The Scriptures," defined Baptists' belief in the Bible as "God's revelation of Himself to man." Dr. Rogers repeatedly reminded us that this confession was to be "descriptive" as opposed to "prescriptive." This simply meant that we were describing Baptist thought and practice as it is, not as we or anyone else thought it should be.

With the input of theologians, pastors, and laypersons, and guided skillfully by Dr. Rogers, the statement was carefully crafted. We all believed it important not to use technical theological terms that would be unintelligible or confusing to the average Baptist. Rather, we worked diligently to choose language that best and most simply conveyed our beliefs.

Our committee was honored to be given this assignment and to serve in this historic task. When presented on the floor of the convention in Orlando, messengers adopted *The Baptist Faith & Message* 2000 as it was presented with a near unanimous vote. In so doing, Southern Baptists embraced their rich Baptist heritage and bore witness to the holy and inerrant Scriptures. While future generations will be called upon to give their own defense, I believe that our committee fulfilled the charge given to us for our day and hour.

In light of the historical importance of this document to Southern Baptists, I enthusiastically welcome this study of *The Baptist Faith & Message* by Rob Phillips. It will be extremely helpful in articulating and understanding why certain changes were necessary and why certain language was chosen. The friendly study-guide format holds readers' attention and challenges them to carefully think through our doctrinal convictions. It can also be easily utilized for churches, as members examine Scripture as the basis of Baptist faith and practice. The author brings his expertise to each chapter and affirms the truth of our long-held convictions. I pray the Holy Spirit will use this book and our doctrinal confession to continue giving "a defense for the hope that is in us."

Susie Hawkins
Member, *The Baptist Faith & Message* 2000 Committee
April 30, 2022

The BF&M is best described as a
confession – a statement of how
Southern Baptists understand
Scripture and all it reveals about
life and godliness.

Introduction

What is The Baptist Faith & Message?

During the 2021 Annual Meeting of Missouri Baptists in Branson, Missouri, messengers adopted a resolution encouraging all Missouri Baptist pastors "to consistently provide instruction to their congregations on the content of the Baptist Faith and Message 2000."

The resolution cited general unfamiliarity with *The Baptist Faith & Message* (BF&M). It also said agreement on the gospel and the core doctrines of our faith is essential both for unity and effective Great Commission work. Finally, the resolution noted that the BF&M 2000 is "the accepted guiding statement of faith for the Southern Baptist Convention."[1]

We offer the following study in support of this resolution. At the same time, we believe the confessional statements in the BF&M are vital, not only to Missouri Baptists, but to all Southern Baptists and our cooperative work of obeying the Great Commission. Our goal is to help pastors and other church leaders equip their members to understand the biblical truths that unite us as Southern Baptists.

A Confessional Statement

Simply put, *The Baptist Faith & Message* 2000 is a statement of beliefs that Southern Baptists hold in common. These beliefs are expressed in eighteen articles of faith, ranging from The Scriptures (Article I) to The Family (Article XVIII). Copies of the BF&M 2000 are available for viewing and downloading online at bfm.sbc.net and in booklet form at Lifeway.com.

The BF&M is best described as a *confession* – a statement of how Southern Baptists understand Scripture and all it reveals about life and godliness. Put another way, the BF&M features valuable summaries of biblical doctrines.

From the earliest days of Christianity, followers of Jesus have valued the ability to articulate the gospel message simply and positively. As the apostle Paul exhorts Timothy, "Fight the good fight of the faith. Take hold of eternal life to which you were called and about which you have made *a good confession* in the presence of many witnesses" (1 Tim. 6:12, emphasis added).

We don't consider the BF&M a *creed* because we don't want to leave the impression it is somehow binding on Southern Baptists, or that it stands alongside, or above, Scripture. As Herschel Hobbs, chairman of the BF&M 1963 committee, writes, "Baptists have always shied away from anything that resembled a creed or a statement of beliefs to which their people were forced to subscribe."

Even so, confessional statements like the BF&M enjoy widespread acceptance by Southern Baptists, which, says Hobbs, "demonstrates that, despite their doctrinal differences here and there, they are a people united in their faith in the basic body of beliefs commonly held by Baptists."[2]

As the introduction to the BF&M 2000 states, "Baptists are a people of deep beliefs and cherished doctrines. Throughout our history we have been a confessional people, adopting statements of faith as a witness to our beliefs and a pledge of our faithfulness to the doctrines revealed in Holy Scripture."

The introduction continues: "Our confessions of faith are rooted in historical precedent, as the church in every age has been called upon to define and defend its beliefs. Each generation of Christians bears the responsibility of guarding the treasury of truth that has been entrusted to us [2 Timothy 1:14] ...."[3]

A Contemporary Response

Southern Baptists introduced the BF&M in 1925 in response to a growing trend of anti-supernaturalism, as well as the fundamentalist-modernist controversy that began in the Northern Presbyterian Church and spread to other denominations.[4] The BF&M was a revised edition of the New Hampshire Confession of Faith, which Baptists nationwide commonly employed.

In 1963, Southern Baptists replied to attacks on the authority and truthfulness of Scripture by adopting revisions to the BF&M. In 1969, Southern Baptists adopted a motion encouraging the agencies, boards, and institutions of the convention to use the BF&M as a guideline in employment, editorial content, and policy.

In 1998, the convention added an article on the family, thus answering cultural confusion about marriage and family with the clear teachings of God's word.

In 1999, SBC President Paige Patterson appointed a blue-ribbon task force to review the 1963 BF&M. Adrian Rogers, pastor of Bellevue Baptist Church in Memphis, and former three-time SBC president, served as chairman. The task force embraced the 1925 and 1963 editions, and recommended some revisions, resulting in the BF&M 2000.

It's important to note that the BF&M 2000 neither subtracts from nor deletes original text. The foundational beliefs of Southern Baptists have remained firmly grounded in Scripture.

At the same time, the 2000 edition features some clarifications and additions. For example, Article VI (The Church) makes it clear that only men may serve as pastors, and Article VII (Baptism and the Lord's Supper) clarifies baptism as an act of obedience, and the Lord's Supper as a memorial to Christ's death – statements lacking in the original document.

Article XII (Education) provides additional details on the responsibilities of teachers in Christian schools, colleges, and seminaries. And Article XV (The Christian and the Social Order) responds to the expansion of legalized abortion and a growing interest in euthanasia in the U.S. by adding: "We should speak on behalf of the unborn and contend for the sanctity of all human life from conception to natural death."

Most significantly, perhaps, is the addition of Article XVIII (The Family), as well as the expansion of Scripture citations at the end of each article – nearly double the number in the BF&M 1925.

See Appendix 1 for a side-by-side comparison of the 1925, 1963, and 2000 editions.

Nature and Function of Confessional Statements

It may prove helpful to note the following statements about the nature and function of statements of faith, taken from the 1925 report to the Southern Baptist Convention:

1. That they [statements of faith like the BF&M] constitute a consensus of opinion of some Baptist body, large or small, for the general instruction and guidance of our own people and others concerning those articles of the Christian faith which are most surely conditions of salvation revealed in the New Testament, viz., repentance towards God and faith in Jesus Christ as Saviour and Lord.

2. That we do not regard them as complete statements of our faith, having any quality of finality or infallibility. As in the past so in the future Baptists should hold themselves free to revise their statements of faith as may seem to them wise and expedient at any time.

3. That any group of Baptists, large or small, have the inherent right to draw up for themselves and publish to the world a confession of their faith whenever they may think it advisable to do so.

4. That the sole authority for faith and practice among Baptists is the Scriptures of the Old and New Testaments. Confessions are only guides in interpretation, having no authority over the conscience.

5. That they are statements of religious convictions, drawn from the Scriptures, and are not to be used to hamper freedom of thought or investigation in other realms of life.[5]

The introduction to the 1963 edition of the BF&M states: "Baptists emphasize the soul's competency before God, freedom in religion, and the priesthood of the believer. However, this emphasis should not be interpreted to mean that there is an absence of certain definite doctrines that Baptists believe, cherish, and with which they have been and are now closely identified."[6]

Baptist churches, associations, state conventions, and other networks have adopted similar statements of faith as a witness to the world and as instruments of doctrinal accountability. As one example, every member of the MBC missionary staff must affirm the BF&M 2000 as a condition of employment. Further, Missouri Baptists who serve on their state convention's executive board, or on other MBC boards and committees, must affirm the BF&M 2000.

As the BF&M 2000 committee expressed, "We are not embarrassed to state before the world that these are doctrines we hold precious and as essential to the Baptist tradition of faith and practice."[7]

"Scripture in its entirety is free from
all falsehood, fraud, or deceit."

– *The Chicago Statement
on Biblical Inerrancy*

Article I

The Scriptures

The Bible is God's revelation of himself to man and is a perfect treasure of divine instruction.

Article I of *The Baptist Faith & Message* 2000 reads:

 The Holy Bible was written by men divinely inspired and is God's revelation of Himself to man. It is a perfect treasure of divine instruction. It has God for its author, salvation for its end, and truth, without any mixture of error, for its matter. Therefore, all Scripture is totally true and trustworthy. It reveals the principles by which God judges us, and therefore is, and will remain to the end of the world, the true center of Christian union, and the supreme standard by which all human conduct, creeds, and religious opinions should be tried. All Scripture is a testimony to Christ, who is Himself the focus of divine revelation.

Comparing 1925/1963/2000

⇒ Article I of the BF&M 1925, Article I of the BF&M 1963, and Article I of the BF&M 2000 are quite similar.

⇒ The 1963 edition adds that the Bible is "the record of God's revelation of Himself to man." It closes with a further addition: "The criterion by which the Bible is to be interpreted is Jesus Christ." Many Southern Baptists came to believe this statement was theologically liberal, or at least vague, and needed to be corrected.

⇒ The BF&M 2000 addresses this challenge with the addition of two statements: "Therefore, all Scripture is totally true and trustworthy," and, "All Scripture is a testimony to Christ, who is Himself the focus of divine revelation."[1]

⇒ See Appendix 1 for a side-by-side comparison.

Four Key Truths

We know the Bible as the word of God. That means God is the source of Scripture, revealing truths we are incapable of knowing without divine help. The Bible is *special revelation* in that it is a record of God's work before time, in time, and beyond time, with a particular emphasis on creation, sin, redemption, and restoration.

As such, Scripture complements God's *general revelation*, which all people witness in creation and conscience (Rom. 1:18-32; 2:14-16).

Let's break down Article I of the BF&M by briefly exploring four key truths Southern Baptists embrace with respect to the Scriptures.

First, the Bible is *inspired*. The apostle Paul writes, "All Scripture is inspired by God" (2 Tim. 3:16). The phrase "inspired by God" comes from the Greek word *theopneustos*. It means "God-breathed" and conveys the idea that Scripture is the product of a holy exhalation.

God did not breathe *into* the Scriptures, thus inspiring them; he breathed *out* his word. The Bible's origin is God himself.

Theologian Charles Ryrie defines inspiration this way: "God superintended the human authors of the Bible so that they composed and recorded without error His message to mankind in the words of their original writings."[2]

By superintendence, we do not mean that God dictated his word to human stenographers, as Muhammad claimed of the Qur'an (via the angel Gabriel). Rather, God breathed out his word, enabling the human authors to use their own writing styles, backgrounds, and experiences to put in written form the very thoughts of God, thus ensuring their accuracy.

Second, the autographs, or originals, of Scripture are *inerrant*. The inerrancy of Scripture means the Bible is fully truthful in all of its teachings. We refer to the original manuscripts, not copies, as inerrant. Subsequent manuscript copies may not claim inerrancy, although we have a treasure trove of manuscripts that give us confidence the Scriptures have been faithfully preserved and carefully copied.

P. D. Feinberg writes that inerrancy is "the view that when all the facts become known, they will demonstrate that the Bible in its original manuscripts and correctly interpreted is entirely true and never false in all it affirms, whether that relates to doctrine or ethics or to the social, physical, or life sciences."[3]

The Chicago Statement on Biblical Inerrancy puts it this way: "Scripture in its entirety is free from all falsehood, fraud, or deceit."[4]

Third, the autographs of Scripture are *infallible*. By infallibility, we mean the original manuscripts are incapable of error. This is because the Bible is inspired, or God-breathed, resulting in "autographs" that are inerrant and infallible.

If the Holy Spirit is the author of Scripture, and his breathed-out words are exactly what he wanted to communicate to us, then we can rightly say these autographs are incapable of error because God is wholly dependable. He does not lie, make mistakes, or lead us astray.

Infallibility may be distinguished from inerrancy but not separated from it. Inerrancy essentially refers to the original manuscripts, while infallibility leans heavily on the character of their divine author.

If the autographs of Scripture contain errors, then the Holy Spirit either does not know all things or is not capable of ensuring that his breathed-out word is recorded accurately.

Infallibility assures us that the God who reveals himself in creation, conscience, Christ, and the canon of Scripture is perfect in all his ways.

Fourth, the Bible is *sufficient*. By sufficient, we mean the Bible is the supreme authority in all matters of doctrine and practice. It's what the Reformers called *sola scriptura* – by Scripture alone.

As Wayne Grudem writes, "The sufficiency of Scripture means that Scripture contained all the words of God he intended his people to have at each state of redemptive history, and that it now contains all the words of God we need for salvation, for trusting him perfectly, and for obeying him perfectly."[5]

In practical terms, this means the Bible answers life's most important questions, such as: Is there a God? Why do I exist? What's wrong with the world? And what happens when I die?

We don't need the Bible plus the Book of Mormon, for example, or the Bible plus the writings of Mary Baker Eddy to answer these questions. The Bible is sufficient.

This doesn't mean Scripture is an exhaustive catalogue of everything God knows, for omniscience cannot be confined to a single set of divinely inspired writings.

Equally important, sufficiency doesn't prevent God from speaking to us today through Spirit-filled leaders, dreams and visions, or even an audible voice if he so chooses, although these forms of communication are better classified as illumination, not revelation, and they must conform to Scripture to be authentic.

Questions for Personal or Group Study

1. How would you describe your beliefs about the Bible in a few short sentences?

2. What's the difference between *general revelation* and *special revelation?*

3. What are four key truths Southern Baptists embrace with respect to the Scriptures?

4. Which of the following best describes the doctrine of inspiration of the Bible:

   (a) A product of human genius, comparable to the plays of Shakespeare

   (b) Dictation from God to human authors, who mechanically transcribed them

   (c) God's superintendence of human authors so they composed and recorded without error his message to mankind in the words of their original writings

   (d) A divine-human partnership in which God's ideas are true but the words of the human authors are subject to error

5. Mark the following statements true or false:

_____ The Holy Spirit is the divine author of Scripture.

_____ The Greek word *theopneustos* means "God-breathed" and conveys the idea that Scripture is the product of a holy exhalation.

_____ The spiritual ideas in Scripture are true, but the human authors may have gotten historical information and other details wrong.

_____ The inerrancy of Scripture applies to the autographs, or original documents, not to subsequent manuscript copies and translations.

_____ Writings like the Book of Mormon, the Catechism of the Catholic Church, and *The Baptist Faith & Message* 2000 may be considered as authoritative as the Bible.

Notes:

Devotional Prayer

Author of holy Scripture, Revealer of all truth,
Breath of Life who breathed out your word,
help me to know you more intimately
as I discover your divine will more perfectly.
As the Spirit confirms the inspiration of Scripture,
may the Father who adopted me help me plumb its depths
and the Son who redeemed me be my all-consuming focus.
Your word is true – incapable of error
because you are wholly dependable.
May I hide your word in my heart
so I am loathe to sin against you.
And may I be equipped to walk the path of good works
you laid out for me in eternity past.

> *— Gen. 2:7; Ps. 119:11; John 17:17;*
> *Eph. 2:10; 2 Tim. 3:16*

"Listen, Israel: The LORD
our God, the LORD is one."

– Deuteronomy 6:4

Article II
God

There is one living and true God who reveals himself to us in three persons: Father, Son, and Holy Spirit, with distinct personal attributes, but without division of nature, essence, or being.

The first paragraph of Article II of *The Baptist Faith & Message* 2000 reads:

 There is one and only one living and true God. He is an intelligent, spiritual, and personal Being, the Creator, Redeemer, Preserver, and Ruler of the universe. God is infinite in holiness and all other perfections. God is all powerful and all knowing; and His perfect knowledge extends to all things, past, present, and future, including the future decisions of His free creatures. To Him we owe the highest love, reverence, and obedience. The eternal triune God reveals Himself to us as Father, Son, and Holy Spirit, with distinct personal attributes, but without division of nature, essence, or being.

Comparing 1925/1963/2000

⇒ Article II of the 1925 edition of the BF&M reads much the same as the first paragraph in the 1963 and 2000 editions.

⇒ Both the 1963 and 2000 editions add paragraphs on God the Father, God the Son, and God the Holy Spirit. These are examined in the chapters to follow.

⇒ The BF&M 2000 adds the following sentence to the 1963 version: "God is all powerful and all knowing; and His perfect knowledge extends to all things, past, present, and future, including the future decisions of His free creatures."[1]

⇒ See Appendix 1 for a side-by-side comparison.

One Living and True God

The Bible consistently declares there is one living and true God, the self-revealed creator who alone must be loved and worshiped. All other gods are false. The physical depictions of these gods, as carved images or naturally occurring phenomena such as stars and trees, in fact represent demons (see Deut. 32:16-17; 1 Cor. 10:19-20).

Perhaps nowhere is the exclusivity of God stated more clearly than in the *Shema*, an affirmation of Judaism and a declaration of faith in one God. It is the oldest fixed daily prayer in Judaism, recited morning and evening since ancient times. It consists of three biblical passages (Deut. 6:4-9; 11:13-21; Num. 15:37-41), two of which instruct the Israelites to speak of these things "when you lie down and when you get up" (Deut. 6:7; 11:19).

The best-known part of the *Shema* is from the first biblical passage: "Listen, Israel: The LORD our God, the LORD is one. Love the LORD your God with all your heart, with all your soul, and with all your strength" (Deut. 6:4-5).

The prophet Isaiah echoes this cry as he calls the Israelites to return to the Lord. Isaiah 44:6 – 45:25 is a powerful reminder from Yahweh that he alone is God. Consider just a small portion of this passage:

> "This is what the LORD, the King of Israel and its Redeemer, the LORD of Armies, says: I am the first and I am the last. There is no God but me" (44:6).

> "I am the LORD, and there is no other; there is no God but me" (45:5).

The New Testament consistently upholds the theme of one God. To cite but two examples:

> Mark 12:29-30 – In response to a scribe who asks about the greatest commandment, Jesus says, "The most important is Listen, O Israel! The Lord our God, the Lord is one. Love the Lord your God with all your heart, with all your soul, with all your mind, and with all your strength."

> 1 Timothy 2:5-6 – Paul writes, "For there is one God and one mediator between God and humanity, the man Christ Jesus, who gave himself as a ransom for all, a testimony at the proper time."

While the theme of one God runs consistently through Scripture, both the Old and New Testaments offer us increasing light into the existence of this one being in three persons.

J. I. Packer writes that the basic assertion of the doctrine of the Trinity is that the unity of the one God is complex: "The three personal 'substances' (as they are called) are coequal and coeternal centers of self-awareness, each being 'I' in relation to two who are 'you' and each partaking of the full divine essence (the 'stuff' of deity, if we may dare to call it that) along with the other two."[2]

Defining the Trinity

How do we biblically define a term that never appears in the Bible? As Jehovah's Witnesses, Muslims, and others are quick to point out, the word *Trinity* is conspicuously absent from the pages of Scripture. That doesn't mean the doctrine is missing in action.

When we talk about the Trinity, it's important to show how Scripture describes God as one eternal being in three persons. This is not as easy as it sounds, for the Trinity in some respects is a mystery – a revelation of God hidden in times past but revealed progressively from Genesis to Revelation.

But we may begin with a simple definition of the Trinity. The word comes from the Latin *trinitas*, meaning "threeness." We may rightly say *Trinity* is a term used to describe the one living and true God, who exists as three distinct, but inseparable, co-equal, co-eternal persons: Father, Son, and Holy Spirit.

Christian apologist Freddy Davis notes, "The Father, Son, and Holy Spirit are all part of the single being who is God, but are also three separate centers of consciousness within that single God who are able to interact with one another in a legitimate personal relationship."[3]

It may advance our understanding to distinguish between *being* and *person*. As the late Nabeel Qureshi, a former Muslim, explains, "Your being is the quality that makes you *what* you are, but your person is the quality that makes you *who* you are."[4] For example, if someone asks who you are, you don't reply, "I'm a human being." You respond by sharing your name, which identifies you as a person.

When we say God is triune, then, we are describing the *what* of God. When we speak of the Father, Son, and Holy Spirit, we are referring to the *who* of God – three persons, indivisible in substance and nature, but distinct in identity.

Questions for Personal or Group Study

1. Read Deuteronomy 6:4-9; 11:13-21; Num. 15:37-41. What is the *Shema*? Why is it important to our understanding of one living and true God?

2. What do carved and chiseled images of gods really represent? Refer to Deut. 32:16-17; 1 Cor. 10:19-20.

3. Which of the following is a biblically faithful definition of the Trinity:

   (a) One God in three parts: Father, Son, and Holy Spirit

   (b) One living and true God, who exists as three distinct, but inseparable, co-equal, co-eternal persons: Father, Son, and Holy Spirit

   (c) Three Gods who are united in purpose

   (d) One God in one person. This person sometimes reveals himself as Father; sometimes as Son; and sometimes as Holy Spirit.

4. The word *Trinity* is not found in Scripture. So, why do we believe in the Trinity?

5. According to Rodrick Durst in *Reordering the Trinity*, there are seventy-five Trinitarian references in the New Testament. Look up the following examples and identify the correct order in which the Father, Son, and Holy Spirit are listed (hint: the Father isn't always named first):

	Order
Matthew 28:19-20	
Romans 8:1-3	
2 Corinthians 13:14 (13:13 in CSB)	
Galatians 4:6	
1 John 4:2	
Jude 20	

Devotional Prayer

Three in One, One in Three,
God of my salvation,
Heavenly Father, blessed Son, eternal Spirit,
I adore thee as one Being, one Essence,
one God in three distinct Persons,
for bringing sinners to thy knowledge and to thy kingdom ...
O Triune God, who commandeth the universe,
thou hast commanded me to ask for those things
that concern thy kingdom and my soul.
Let me live and pray as one baptized
into the threefold Name.[5]

"... the Eternal One of Israel does not
lie or change his mind, for he is not
a man who changes his mind."

– *1 Samuel 15:29*

Article II-A
God the Father

God the Father is the first person of the Trinity. He is a divine, eternal, non-human person who is immortal and invisible. He adopts believing sinners as his sons and daughters.

Article II-A of *The Baptist Faith & Message* 2000 reads:

 God as Father reigns with providential care over His universe, His creatures, and the flow of the stream of human history according to the purposes of His grace. He is all powerful, all knowing, all loving, and all wise. God is Father in truth to those who become children of God through faith in Jesus Christ. He is fatherly in His attitude toward all men.

Comparing 1925/1963/2000

⇒ Article II-A of the 1963 and 2000 editions of the BF&M does not appear in the 1925 version.

⇒ The 1963 and 2000 editions of this article essentially read the same, with the exception that the BF&M 2000 adds the words "all knowing" to the second sentence.[1]

⇒ See Appendix 1 for a side-by-side comparison.

The Father is a Person but Not a Man

There is little dispute among professing Christians that our Heavenly Father is God. But if we fail to understand the Father correctly, and if we miss the clear teachings of Scripture with respect to his relationship with the other members of the Godhead, then the biblical doctrines of creation, redemption, and restoration suffer as well.

It's important to note while the Father is a *person*, he is not human. Balaam – a scoundrel who prophesies for hire – nevertheless speaks the truth concerning God's unchanging decrees when he says, "God is not a man, that he might lie, or a son of man, that he might change his mind. Does he speak and not act, or promise and not fulfill?" (Num. 23:19).

On another occasion, the prophet Samuel informs Saul that the Lord has torn away the kingship of Israel from Saul and given it to David. "Furthermore," he says, "the Eternal One of Israel does not lie or change his mind, for he is not man who changes his mind" (1 Sam. 15:29). Other Old Testament passages make similar claims (Job 9:32; Isa. 31:2; Hos. 11:9).

The Father is a divine, eternal, non-human person who is immortal and invisible.

In the New Testament, when Peter declares Jesus the Christ, the Son of the living God, Jesus says to the disciple, "Blessed are you, Simon son of Jonah, because flesh and blood did not reveal this to you, but my Father in heaven" (Matt. 16:17). No human being revealed the truth to Peter. It was the Father in heaven.

Not only does Scripture deny the humanity of the Father; it affirms his divine, eternal nature as spirit. Jesus tells a Samaritan woman that "an hour is coming, and is now here, when the true worshipers will worship the Father in Spirit and in truth. Yes, the Father wants such people to worship him. God is spirit, and those who worship him must worship in Spirit and in truth" (John 4:23-24).

When the Bible tells us that no one has seen God, it's a reference to the Father, who is spirit (John 1:18; 4:24). Paul declares that Jesus is "the image of the invisible God" (Col. 1:15). The writer of Hebrews describes Jesus as "the radiance [or reflection] of God's glory and the exact expression of his nature" (Heb. 1:3). Jesus puts it more plainly when he tells Philip, "The one who has seen me has seen the Father" (John 14:9).

To summarize: The Father is a divine, eternal, non-human person who is immortal and invisible.

The Fatherhood of God

Now, let's look at several ways the Bible describes the fatherhood of God.

First, the Greek word *theos* is used of the Father. We see this in numerous passages, such as Galatians 1:1 and 1 Peter 1:2. While *theos* also is used of Satan (2 Cor. 4:4) and pagan idols (1 Cor. 8:5), the New Testament writers are clear that these entities are not God by nature (Gal. 4:8). In fact, Paul argues that the gods of the pagans actually are demons (1 Cor. 10:20).

Second, the Father's divine attributes reveal his deity. The Father possesses eternal power (Rom. 1:20; 1 Tim. 6:16). He is almighty (Rev. 19:6); immortal (1 Tim. 1:17); all-knowing (Matt. 6:32); perfect (Matt. 5:48); and true deity (John 17:3).

Third, the Father performs the works of God. These include

creation (Heb. 2:10); sovereignty (Matt. 11:25); providence (Matt. 5:45; 6:26); the authority to judge (John 5:22); the bestowing of life (John 5:21, 26); and salvation (Eph. 1:4).

Fourth, the Father speaks the words of God. In Romans 1, Paul claims he is "called as an apostle and set apart for the gospel of God – which he [the Father] promised beforehand through his prophets in the Holy Scriptures – concerning his Son, Jesus Christ ...." (vv. 1-3). And in Hebrews 1, the writer declares, "Long ago God spoke to the fathers by the prophets at different times and in different ways. In these last days, he has spoken to us by his Son ...." (vv. 1-2).

Fifth, the Father is worshiped as God. We are to "ascribe to the LORD the glory due his name; worship the LORD in the splendor of his holiness" (Ps. 29:2); "worship and bow down" (Ps. 95:6); and "worship the Father in Spirit and in truth" (John 4:23).

Sixth, Jesus declares the fatherhood of God. For Jesus, "God" and "Heavenly Father" are synonymous expressions. Jesus clearly has the Father in mind in many references to God. For example, as he is nailed to a cross and hoisted between two criminals, Jesus prays, "Father, forgive them, because they do not know what they are doing" (Luke 23:34). Then, just before he breathes his last, Jesus shouts, "Father, into your hands I entrust my spirit" (Luke 23:46).

Seventh, the Bible reveals God as the father of all humanity. Scripture shows Yahweh to be the father of all people through creation. Humans are fashioned in God's image, so to the extent that we are his creatures, he is our father (see Acts 17:28-29).

Questions for Personal or Group Study

1. Why do we say God the Father is a person but not a man? Consider Numbers 23:19; 1 Samuel 15:29; Job 9:32; Isaiah 31:2; and Hosea 11:9.

2. Read Matthew 16:13-20. Who reveals the truth about Jesus to Peter?

3. Mark the following statements about God the Father as true or false:

_____ He existed before Jesus.

_____ He has a body of flesh and bones.

_____ He is co-equal and co-eternal with the Son and the Holy Spirit.

_____ For Jesus, "God" and "Heavenly Father" are synonymous expressions.

_____ The Bible reveals God as the father of all humanity, but only those who trust in Jesus are the Father's adopted sons and daughters.

4. In what way is God the Father to be understood as the father of Jesus?

5. Match the following Scripture passages with the divine attributes of the Father:

Matthew 5:48	Eternal power
Matthew 6:32	Almighty
John 17:3	Immortal
Romans 1:20	All-knowing
1 Timothy 1:17	Perfect
Revelation 19:6	True deity

Notes:

Devotional Prayer

Father of all creation, I stand amazed
when I consider thy heavens and the work of thy fingers.
Father of Abraham, I am staggered
that you would enter into a covenant
with a man without a country,
resulting in eternal blessings for me.
Father of Israel, I am humbled
that you created a great nation
from the least of the earth's peoples.
Father of the Lord Jesus Christ, I cannot fathom
the depths of your love in sacrificing your Son to rescue me.
Father of the church, I am forever blessed
by my adoption into your eternal family.
Abba, Father, Dearest Daddy,
hold my hand and tell me once again
how you loved me from the foundation of the world.

— *Gen. 12:1-3; Deut. 7:7; Ps. 8:3; Rom. 8:15-16;*
2 Cor. 1:3; Gal. 4:4-7; Eph. 1:4

"The Word became flesh
and dwelt among us."

– John 1:14

Article II-B
God the Son

Jesus is the eternal Son of God who, in the Incarnation, set aside his privileged position at the Father's right hand (but not his deity) in order to become a human being who rescued us from sin by becoming sin for us on the cross.

Article II-B of *The Baptist Faith & Message* 2000 reads:

 Christ is the eternal Son of God. In His incarnation as Jesus Christ He was conceived of the Holy Spirit and born of the virgin Mary. Jesus perfectly revealed and did the will of God, taking upon Himself human nature with its demands and necessities and identifying Himself completely with mankind yet without sin. He honored the divine law by His personal obedience, and in His substitutionary death on the cross He made provision for the redemption of men from sin. He was raised from the dead with a glorified body and appeared to His disciples as the person who was with them before His crucifixion. He ascended into heaven and is now exalted at the right hand of God where He is the One Mediator, fully God, fully man, in whose Person is effected the reconciliation between God and man. He will return in power and glory to judge the world and to consummate His redemptive mission. He now dwells in all believers as the living and ever present Lord.

Comparing 1925/1963/2000

⇒ Article II-B of the 1963 and 2000 editions of the BF&M does not appear in the 1925 version.

⇒ Article II-B of the BF&M 1963 and Article II-B of the BF&M 2000 essentially read the same, with some minor differences.

⇒ One difference should be noted. The 1963 version reads: "He ascended into heaven and is now exalted at the right hand of God where He is the One Mediator, *partaking of the nature of God and of man* ...." The BF&M 2000 substitutes the last phrase (italicized for emphasis) with "fully God, fully man."[1]

⇒ See Appendix 1 for a side-by-side comparison.

The Word Became Flesh

Simply stated, the doctrine of the Incarnation means the eternal Son of God took on human flesh in the person of Jesus of Nazareth. As such, Jesus is one person in two natures: divine and human. As the apostle John writes, "The Word became flesh and dwelt among us" (John 1:14).

The importance of this truth should not be overlooked. If Jesus is not divine, he cannot be our redeemer; if he is not human, he cannot be our mediator.

The doctrine of the Incarnation flows naturally from a biblical understanding of the Trinity. Historic Christianity affirms belief in one infinitely perfect, eternal, and personal God, the transcendent creator and sovereign sustainer of the universe. This one God is triune, existing eternally and simultaneously as three distinct, but not separate, persons: Father, Son, and Holy Spirit.

In this light, Jesus clearly may be seen as the eternal Son of God who, in the Incarnation, set aside his privileged position at the Father's right hand (but not his deity) in order to become a sinless human being who rescued us from sin by becoming sin for us on the cross (2 Cor. 5:21).

Christ's Deity

The New Testament writers consistently affirm the deity of Christ, calling him God (John 1:1), the creator (John 1:3; Col. 1:16), and equating him with the Father (Heb. 1:3). In response to those who say that Jesus never claimed to be God, consider:

1. Jesus uses the divine expression *I AM*, echoing God's self-revelation to Moses in the burning bush (e.g., John 8:24, 28, 58; cf. Exod. 3).

2. Jesus claims equality with God (John 5:18; 10:30; 17:5).

3. Jesus receives worship (Matt. 28:17; John 20:28).

4. Jesus forgives sins (Mark 2:1-12).

5. Jesus teaches with divine authority (Mark 1:21-22; John 8:13-20; 12:49-50).

6. Jesus affirms the apostles' statements about his deity. That is, he promises the apostles that the Holy Spirit will guide them into all truth and bring to their minds the things he says and does. In effect, he confirms in advance what they write later (John 1:1-3, 14; Col. 1:15-16; 2:9; Phil. 2:5-11; Heb. 1:1-4).

7. Jesus demonstrates the attributes unique to God: omniscience (John 16:30); omnipotence (Matt. 28:18); omnipresence (Matt.

28:20); eternality (John 1:1); immutability (Heb. 13:8); and divine authority (John 5:22). Even the Father calls Jesus God (Heb. 1:8).

Christ's Humanity

If the Incarnation means that Jesus is completely divine and completely human at the same time, never surrendering one nature to the other, how might we explain the apparent absence of divine attributes at certain times in our Savior's life?

For example, why doesn't Jesus know the day and hour of his return? Why does he get tired, thirsty, and hungry? And why does he insist that the Father is greater than he is?

Theologian Bruce Ware provides marvelous insight into the two natures of Christ in *The Man Christ Jesus*. He begins with Philippians 2:5-8, which expresses the self-emptying of the eternal Son as he takes on human nature.

"To obey to the point of death requires the ability to die, and for this, Jesus had to be human."

– Bruce Ware

First, Ware notes that Paul expresses no doubts about the deity of Christ. The phrase "though he was in the form of God" (v. 6) means Jesus exists in very nature as God, with the inner divine substance that is God's alone.

Second, when Paul writes that Christ "did not count equality with God a thing to be grasped" (v. 6), he means that Jesus did not cling to his privileged position at the Father's right hand, or to the rights and prerogatives that go along with full equality with the Father. Instead, he fulfilled his mission as the servant of all.

Third, Jesus "emptied himself, by taking the form of a servant" (v. 7). The Greek *ekenosen* means Christ "poured out himself." In other words, all of Christ, as eternal God, is poured out. As Jesus becomes human, he loses nothing of his divine nature.

Fourth, Jesus "humbled himself by becoming obedient to the point of death, even death on a cross" (v. 8). Ware notes, "To obey to the point of death requires the ability to die, and for this, Jesus had to be human."[2]

So, when we come to passages that tell us Jesus doesn't know something, or gets hungry or thirsty, or dies, we may understand that Jesus neither surrenders his deity nor abandons his claims of divinity. Rather, he chooses, in certain instances, not to avail himself of certain divine attributes so that he might fully identify with sinful and fallen human beings.

As the writer of Hebrews puts it, "he had to be like his brothers and sisters in every way, so that he could become a merciful and faithful high priest in matters pertaining to God, to make atonement for the sins of the people" (Heb. 2:17).

Questions for Personal or Group Study

1. How would you describe the doctrine of the Incarnation in simple terms?

2. Match the following Scripture passages with Christ's claims of deity:

Matthew 28:18	Receives worship
Mark 2:1-12	Uses divine expression *I AM*
John 8:13-20	Forgives sins
John 8:58	Claims omnipotence
John 10:30	Teaches with divine authority
John 20:28	Claims equality with the Father

3. If Jesus is fully divine throughout his earthly ministry, why are there times he suffers the frailties of humanity – not knowing certain details, getting tired, hungry, or thirsty, for example?

4. Read Philippians 2:5-8. What do these verses tell us about Jesus the God-Man?

5. Which of the following statements about Jesus is *false?*

(a) Jesus is the eternal Son of God.

(b) Jesus added sinless humanity to his deity via the miracle of the virgin birth.

(c) Jesus became a human being and retains his physical body in heaven today.

(d) Jesus became a sinner on the cross.

(e) When Jesus became human, he lost nothing of his divine nature.

Devotional Prayer

Dearest Son of God and Son of Man,
help me to adopt the same attitude as yours,
for you, who existed in the form of God,
did not consider equality with God
as something to be exploited.
Instead, you emptied yourself –
poured out your divinity into human skin –
and assumed the form of a servant,
taking on the likeness of humanity.
And when you had come as a man,
you humbled yourself by becoming obedient
to the point of death – even to death on a cross.
May I, too, be humble, obedient, and willing
to take up my cross daily and follow you.

— Luke 9:23; Phil. 2:5-8

Article II-C
God the Holy Spirit

The Holy Spirit is the third person of the Trinity. He is both divine and personal, co-equal and co-eternal with the Father and the Son, and he is a full partner within the Godhead in creation, redemption, and the revealing of Scripture.

Article II-C of *The Baptist Faith & Message* 2000 reads:

 The Holy Spirit is the Spirit of God, fully divine. He inspired holy men of old to write the Scriptures. Through illumination He enables men to understand truth. He exalts Christ. He convicts men of sin, of righteousness, and of judgment. He calls men to the Saviour, and effects regeneration. At the moment of regeneration He baptizes every believer into the Body of Christ. He cultivates Christian character, comforts believers, and bestows the spiritual gifts by which they serve God through His church. He seals the believer unto the day of final redemption. His presence in the Christian is the guarantee that God will bring the believer into the fullness of the stature of Christ. He enlightens and empowers the believer and the church in worship, evangelism, and service.

Comparing 1925/1963/2000

⇒ Article II-C of the 1963 and 2000 editions of the BF&M does not appear in the 1925 version.

⇒ The 1963 and 2000 editions of this article essentially read the same, with some minor differences.

⇒ Comparing the 1963 and 2000 versions, the BF&M 2000 adds the words "fully divine" to the end of the first sentence, and it substitutes the word "guarantee" for "assurance" in describing the sustaining presence of the Holy Spirit in the Christian.

⇒ Finally, the 2000 edition adds this sentence: "At the moment of regeneration He [the Holy Spirit] baptizes every believer into the Body of Christ."[1]

⇒ See Appendix 1 for a side-by-side comparison.

The Forgotten Member of the Trinity

In some ways, the Holy Spirit is the neglected, if not forgotten, member of the Trinity.

The biblical doctrines of foreknowledge, election, predestination, and adoption awaken us to the eternal love of God the Father.

Through the Incarnation, the second person of the triune Godhead becomes flesh and pitches his tent with us (John 1:14). He experiences in full measure what it means to be human, including facing temptation – yet without sinning so that he may clothe us in God's righteousness (2 Cor. 5:21).

Christians are said to have a personal relationship with Jesus Christ and to be the adopted sons and daughters of God the Father.

But where is the Holy Spirit in all of this? As we know from

Scripture, none of the persons of the Godhead acts alone. As such, the Holy Spirit is a co-equal and co-eternal partner in all of the Trinity's work.

So, it's important for us to understand how thoroughly the Bible depicts both the personhood and deity of the Holy Spirit.

The Spirit's Personhood

One of the clearest demonstrations of the Holy Spirit's personality is his use of personal pronouns in reference to himself. Two examples make this plain:

> Acts 10:19-20 – "While Peter was thinking about the vision, the Spirit told him, 'Three men are here looking for you. Get up, go downstairs, and go with them with no doubts at all, because I have sent them.'"

> Acts 13:1-2 – "Now in the church at Antioch there were prophets and teachers: Barnabas, Simeon who was called Niger, Lucius of Cyrene, Manaen, a close friend of Herod the tetrarch, and Saul. As they were worshiping the Lord and fasting, the Holy Spirit said, 'Set apart for me Barnabas and Saul for the work to which I have called them.'"

Note that the Holy Spirit speaks personally to Peter as well as to believers in the Antioch church. These are actions of a sentient being, not an impersonal force.

Jesus also uses personal pronouns to speak of the Holy Spirit, telling his followers, "When the Spirit of truth comes, he will guide you into all the truth. For he will not speak on his own, but he will speak whatever he hears. He will also declare to you what is to come. He will glorify me, because he will take from what is mine and declare it to you" (John 16:13-14).

According to Jesus, the Holy Spirit arrives, guides, discerns the truth, hears and speaks, discloses future events, testifies about Jesus, and glorifies him – all demonstrations of personhood.

Finally, Scripture describes the Spirit's personal activities, which include speaking (Acts 8:29), revealing (Acts 21:11), interceding (Rom. 8:26-27), and distributing spiritual gifts (1 Cor. 12:6, 11). The Spirit also may be blasphemed (Matt. 12:31), grieved (Eph. 4:30), lied to (Acts 5:3-4), and insulted (Heb. 10:28-29).

The Spirit's Deity

What do we see the Spirit doing that only God can do?

For starters, the Holy Spirit creates (Gen. 1:1-2; Ps. 104:30). The Spirit also demonstrates omniscience and omnipresence, displaying qualities that establish him as co-equal and co-eternal with the Father and the Son (Ps. 139:7-8; 1 Cor. 2:10-11).

What's more, the Spirit shares a divine name, symbolic of divine presence, with the other members of the triune Godhead (Matt. 28:19).

The Spirit's role in creation, redemption, and the revealing of Scripture is distinct, yet inseparable, from the work of the other members of the Trinity.

Perhaps the clearest passage that illustrates both the personality and deity of the Holy Spirit is found in Acts 5. After Ananias and Sapphira fraudulently claim to have given the full proceeds of a land sale to the church, Peter confronts Ananias, asking, "[W]hy has Satan filled your heart to lie to the Holy Spirit and keep back part of the proceeds of the land? Wasn't it yours while you possessed it? And after it was sold, wasn't it at your disposal? Why is it that you planned this thing in your heart? You have not lied to people but to God" (vv. 3-4).

To whom did Ananias lie: to the Holy Spirit, or to God? The

answer, of course, is that Ananias lied to both. To lie to the Holy Spirit is to lie to God since the Spirit occupies an equal place in the Trinity with the Father and the Son.

Finally, Paul refers to the Spirit as "Lord," using the Greek word *kyrios* (2 Cor. 3:17-18). This term is applied to other members of the Godhead in the New Testament, and it is the word used to translate the divine name *Yahweh* in the Septuagint, the Greek translation of the Old Testament.

The Bible is replete with references to the personality and deity of the Holy Spirit. A faithful rendering of God's word leads us to the conclusion that the Holy Spirit is an equal partner with the Father and the Son in the Godhead. His role in creation, redemption, and the revealing of Scripture is distinct, yet inseparable, from the work of the other members of the Trinity. None of the divine persons of the Godhead acts alone.

Questions for Personal or Group Study

1. Jehovah's Witnesses depict the Holy Spirit as an impersonal force, referring to him as "holy spirit" (note the lower-case spelling). Muslims believe the Holy Spirit is the angel Gabriel, who delivered the Qur'an to Muhammad. Why are these views of the Spirit incorrect? What is a proper biblical understanding of the Holy Spirit?

2. Why do you think the Holy Spirit is the forgotten member of the Trinity? That is, why do we tend to think of him less often, or consider him the least important person in the Godhead? How should we think of the Spirit in relation to God the Father and Jesus?

3. Mark the following statements true or false:

_____ The Holy Spirit is co-equal and co-eternal with the Father and the Son.

_____ The Holy Spirit refers to himself in Scripture using personal pronouns.

_____ God the Father created the Holy Spirit, and Jesus sent the Spirit to earth at Pentecost.

_____ The Holy Spirit may be sinned against.

_____ The Holy Spirit is like the wind, or even electricity – an impersonal force God uses to accomplish his will.

4. Match the following Scripture passages with the work of the Holy Spirit:

Genesis 1:1-2	Intercedes in prayer
Matthew 28:19	Distributes spiritual gifts
John 16:7-11	Creates
Acts 13:1-2	Convicts unbelievers
Romans 8:26-27	Calls to Christian service
1 Corinthians 12:6, 11	Shares a divine name with the Father and the Son

5. Read Acts 5:1-11. What does this passage tell us about the personhood and deity of the Holy Spirit? Further, what do these verses communicate about the possible consequences of sinning against the Spirit?

Devotional Prayer

O God the Holy Spirit ...
Open my understanding to know the Holy Scriptures;
Reveal to my soul the counsels and works
of the blessed Trinity;
Instill into my dark mind the saving knowledge of Jesus;
Make me acquainted with his covenant undertakings
and his perfect fulfillment of them,
that by resting on his finished work
I may find the Father's love in the Son,
his Father, my Father,
and may be brought through thy influence
to have fellowship with the Three in One.[2]

Article III

Man

Human beings are God's crowning act of creation. By making us in his image, God sets humanity apart from the rest of creation. Therefore, his work of redemption is directed specifically to men and women whose "imago dei" has been tarnished by sin.

Article III of *The Baptist Faith & Message* 2000 reads:

 Man is the special creation of God, made in His own image. He created them male and female as the crowning work of His creation. The gift of gender is thus part of the goodness of God's creation. In the beginning man was innocent of sin and was endowed by his Creator with freedom of choice. By his free choice man sinned against God and brought sin into the human race. Through the temptation of Satan man transgressed the command of God, and fell from his original innocence whereby his posterity inherit a nature and an environment inclined toward sin. Therefore, as soon as they are capable of moral action, they become transgressors and are under condemnation. Only the grace of God can bring man into

His holy fellowship and enable man to fulfill the creative purpose of God. The sacredness of human personality is evident in that God created man in His own image, and in that Christ died for man; therefore, every person of every race possesses full dignity and is worthy of respect and Christian love.

Comparing 1925/1963/2000

⇒ Article III gets progressively longer as we move from the 1925 edition to the 1963 and 2000 versions.

⇒ Article III of the BF&M 1925 is titled, "The Fall of Man."

⇒ The 1925 version quotes Genesis 1:27 and 2:7, while the 1963 and 2000 editions summarize these passages in their first paragraphs.

⇒ While the 1925 edition states that man "was created in a state of holiness under the law of his Maker," the 1963 and 2000 editions say, "In the beginning man was innocent of sin and was endowed by his Creator with freedom of choice."

⇒ The BF&M 2000 adds the following comments to the 1963 version, thus addressing emerging questions about human sexuality:

- "He created them male and female ...."
- "The gift of gender is thus part of the goodness of God's creation."

⇒ Finally, the 2000 edition alters the final sentence as follows:

- 1963 – "... every man possesses dignity and is worthy of respect and Christian love."

- 2000 – "... every person of every race possesses full dignity and is worthy of respect and Christian love."[1]

⇒ See Appendix 1 for a side-by-side comparison.

The *Imago Dei*

God's crowning act of creation occurred when "the LORD God formed the man out of the dust from the ground and breathed the breath of life into his nostrils, and the man became a living being" (Gen. 2:7).

The Bible is a story about God and human beings: Adam and Eve's creation in innocence, their rebellion and fall, and God's work of restoring both sinful mankind and a cursed creation to their Edenic innocence. God's redemptive role in human history may be summarized in several key biblical truths.

First, God has created every human being in his image. All people possess the *imago dei*, or image of God. This doesn't mean we look like God, for God is spirit. It means, however, that all people possess a spiritual capacity that makes us moral creatures who can know God and enjoy intimate fellowship with him.

Every person, regardless of ethnicity, gender, age, abilities, socioeconomic class, or even behavior, retains God-given worth and dignity. The *imago dei* extends to every human being without exception. Therefore, every person is to be treated with the utmost respect.

By making human beings in his image, God sets humanity apart from the rest of creation. No other earthly being – no matter how beautiful, intelligent, or powerful – is able to make this claim, or even conceive such a marvelous truth. God's work of redemption is directed specifically to the salvation of men and women whose *imago dei* has been tarnished by sin.

Second, God's glory is revealed in the distinctions between men and women. Human beings are created male and female – a distinction Jesus affirms (Gen. 1:27; Matt. 19:4-6). Gender reflects the goodness of God's creation, including diversity, unity, and order. Thus, we should rightly celebrate true masculinity and femininity as gifts from God.

Men and women are equal in value and dignity before God – he took Eve from Adam's side, not from Adam's head or feet – and they best glorify God when they carry out the complementary roles he has given them. The gender chaos that prevails in modern society grieves the heart of God.

Third, every human being is fallen. Sin entered the human race through the disobedience of Adam and Eve. It has spread to all humanity, as well as to the created order (Gen. 3). As a result, there is sickness, death, conflict, and a diminished sense of community throughout the world.

All people are born with an inclination to sin, and all people act upon this tendency to live independently of God through willful rebellion against him. This alienates people from God and merits his divine justice (Rom. 3:10, 23; 6:23).

The world is not as God created it or intended it to be. Humanity and the world system in which we live spiral continuously away from God. Sadly, Christians contribute to this malaise as we fall into temptation and sin – often grievously.

Christ is redeeming people from every tribe, tongue, and nation, who stand now and forevermore in the presence of God in unified worship.

Fourth, God has sent his Son to redeem us. Sinful human beings and the fallen world in which we live would spin desperately out of control, with no hope of being restored to a right relationship with our creator, apart from the finished work of Christ. As the eternal Son of God, Jesus left the glory of heaven and came to earth, adding sinless humanity to his deity via the miracle of the virgin birth, on a mission to seek and to save the lost (Luke 19:10).

Jesus' sinless life, sacrificial and substitutionary death on the cross, and physical resurrection from the dead purchased the salvation of all who repent and trust in him – without distinction of ethnicity, gender, age, ability, or social status. This truly is good news for all people, who are called to repent and believe.

Fifth, Christ is redeeming people from every tribe, tongue, and nation, who stand now and forevermore in the presence of God in unified worship (Rev. 5:9-10). Further, Jesus has promised to return to earth to set things right (Matt. 25:31-46; Rev. 22:12).

One day, all people will stand before Jesus and give an account of their lives, including how they treated others (John 5:28-29; Rom. 14:10; 1 Cor. 4:5; Rev. 20:11-15). He then will purge our fallen world of sin and its stain, restoring creation to its pristine perfection, and dwelling personally with those he has saved (2 Pet. 3:10-13; Rev. 21-22).

As the authors of Lifeway's six-part study on *The Baptist Faith & Message* put it, "Only by knowing Jesus Christ can we understand what true humanity was meant to be. By God's grace, demonstrated and made ours in Christ, we are restored to fellowship with God and are enabled to fulfill the purpose for which we were made."[2]

Questions for Personal or Group Study

1. What does the phrase *imago dei* mean, and why is it significant for all human beings?

2. Why does the BF&M 2000 say, "The gift of gender is thus part of the goodness of God's creation"? How should we respond to those who insist that gender is "fluid," or a matter of personal choice? How should we treat those who struggle with gender confusion?

3. Which of the following statements is false:

(a) Every person, regardless of ethnicity, gender, age, abilities, socioeconomic class, or even behavior, retains God-given worth and dignity.

(b) God's glory is revealed in the distinction between males and females.

(c) Adam and Eve were created with a sin nature.

(d) The world is not as God created it or intended it to be.

(e) Christ is redeeming people from every tribe, tongue, and nation.

4. Read Genesis 3 and list as many consequences of the Fall as you can find. Then, take special note of verse 15. What promise does God make that Jesus later fulfills?

5. What does the apostle Peter say Jesus is going to do when he returns (2 Pet. 3:10-13)? How does the apostle John describe the state of human beings in the new heavens and earth (Rev. 21:4)?

Devotional Prayer

O sovereign Creator,
you have made all things and declared them "very good indeed."
According to your divine will and good pleasure,
you formed the man from the dust of the ground
and breathed the breath of life into his nostrils,
and the man became a living being.
You have made all people in the "imago dei"
and designed us to be imagers of your divine glory.
But Adam fell, and we are fallen and in desperate need of
* salvation.*
So, you sent your Son, "the last Adam,"
who poured his deity into sinless humanity,
and offered his perfect life for our redemption.
One day, we will share the unvarnished glory
of the resurrected Christ
and be restored to the sinless glow
in which man and woman basked in the Garden of Eden.
Lord, these promises cause us to echo the words of the psalmist,
"When I observe your heavens,
the work of your fingers,
the moon and the stars,
which you set in place,
what is a human being that you remember him,
a son of man that you look after him?"

— Gen. 1:31; 2:7; Ps. 8:3-4; 1 Cor. 15:45

Article IV

Salvation

Salvation is God's remedy for the sin that has ruined everything and alienated everyone from him.

Article IV of *The Baptist Faith & Message* 2000 begins:

 Salvation involves the redemption of the whole man, and is offered freely to all who accept Jesus Christ as Lord and Saviour, who by His own blood obtained eternal redemption for the believer. In its broadest sense salvation includes regeneration, justification, sanctification, and glorification. There is no salvation apart from personal faith in Jesus Christ as Lord.

Comparing 1925/1963/2000

⇒ Article IV of the BF&M 1925 is titled, "The Way of Salvation." It reads differently than the opening paragraph of the 1963 and 2000 editions, but its content is consistent with the later versions.

⇒ The BF&M 1925 deals with key elements of salvation in

separate articles: Article V: Justification; Article VI: The Freeness of Salvation; Article VII: Regeneration; Article VIII: Repentance and Faith; Article IX: God's Purpose of Grace; Article X: Sanctification; and Article XI: Perseverance. These articles do not align numerically with the articles of the 1963 and 2000 editions of the BF&M but are addressed in them, as we see later.

⇒ Article IV of the BF&M 1963 includes paragraphs on regeneration, repentance and faith / justification, sanctification, and glorification.

⇒ Article IV of the BF&M 2000 covers the same elements of salvation as seen in the 1963 edition but numbers them differently.

⇒ In future chapters, we match, as best we're able, similar paragraphs concerning salvation between the 1925, 1963, and 2000 editions of the BF&M.[1]

⇒ See Appendix 1 for a side-by-side comparison.

God's Remedy for Sin

People use the words *salvation* and *saved* in a variety of settings, from sporting events to political campaigns to natural disasters. Even within Christian circles, there is disagreement as to what it means to be saved and how salvation is acquired. So, it's critical for us to begin with a definition.

Stated simply, salvation is God's remedy for the sin that has ruined everything and alienated everyone from him. The Lord reveals this remedy as soon as Adam and Eve rebel against him. He promises a future redeemer who crushes the head of Satan (Gen. 3:15). Then, the Lord provides additional promises throughout the Old Testament, granting us more than four hundred prophecies, appearances, or foreshadows of the Messiah.[2]

Jesus of Nazareth bursts onto the scene at just the right time (Gal. 4:4). He lives a sinless life and dies on a Roman cross, taking upon himself our sins and paying the penalty of death for them (2 Cor. 5:21). Then, he rises physically from the dead on the third day, conquering Satan, sin, and death, and freely offering forgiveness of sins and everlasting life by grace through faith in him.

Before ascending into heaven, Jesus promises to return one day to fulfill all things – that is, to complete his work of salvation, judge every person, and set everything right.

Deliverance from Danger

The concept of salvation comes from the Hebrew word *yasa*, which means "to be wide or roomy." It's often rendered "to save, rescue, deliver." The word *salvation* is used in many ways throughout the Old and New Testaments, and it's important to consider the context to determine the proper application.

For example, the words *save* and *salvation* often refer to physical, not spiritual, deliverance. In the Old Testament, people are saved from enemies on the battlefield (Deut. 20:4). Daniel is rescued from the mouth of the lion (Dan. 6:20). And the righteous are delivered from the wicked (Ps. 7:10; 59:2).

In the New Testament, the Lord delivers Paul from shipwreck (Acts 27:22, 31, 34). In other passages, salvation in the physical sense refers to being taken from danger to safety, or even vindication (Phil. 1:19) and from disease to health (Jas. 5:15).

Of course, the greatest type of salvation is holistic in nature, involving the spiritual as well as the physical aspects of the whole person. God sends his Son to be the Savior of the world (1 John 4:14). Jesus comes to seek and to save lost sinners (Luke 19:10). Because of his finished work on the cross, those who call upon the name of the Lord are saved (Rom. 10:13).

This salvation comes by the grace of God through faith in Christ (Eph. 2:8-9). While the Lord has saved us from the penalty of sin, he is working, even now, to save us from sin's power (Rom. 5:10; Heb. 7:25; Jas. 1:21). One day, God's work of salvation is complete, when the very presence of sin is eradicated (Rom. 13:11; 1 Pet. 1:9). These wonderful truths prompt the writer of Hebrews to exhort followers of Jesus not to neglect the great salvation given to us (Heb. 2:3).

An Unbreakable Relationship

For followers of Jesus, salvation is experienced as an everlasting, unbreakable relationship with him. It has both temporal and eternal benefits. In fact, of the many terms the Bible uses to describe salvation, several cannot be confined to time or expressed in chronological order. Consider, for example, that we are *foreknown*, *elected*, and *predestined* in eternity past. Put another way, we are saved before time began.

Other elements of salvation are experienced personally within our lifetimes as God *calls* us to himself; *regenerates* us, or makes us spiritually alive; *justifies* us, or declares us in right standing with him; *indwells* us, or takes up permanent residence in our human spirits; *baptizes* us in the Holy Spirit, or places us positionally into the church; *sanctifies* us, or sets us apart and begins the process of making us more like Christ; *adopts* us into his family; and *seals* us, or places his mark of ownership on us.

One day, the final act of salvation is completed in *glorification*. We are physically resurrected and given incorruptible bodies similar to the resurrected body of our Savior.

Since Christians possess a relationship with Christ, which already has begun and extends into eternity future, it is biblically faithful to say we *were saved* (from the penalty of sin), *are being saved* (from the power of sin), and *will be saved* (from the presence of sin). The Lord alone applies these marvelous elements of salvation to our lives.

Please keep in mind these are not separate works that God cobbles together. Rather, they are elements of a unified whole.

Questions for Personal or Group Study

1. How would you describe God's work of salvation in simple terms?

2. The words *save* and *salvation* often refer to physical, not spiritual, deliverance in Scripture. Look up the following passages and identify *who* is being saved and *from what* they are being delivered:

	Who?	*From what?*
Deuteronomy 20:4		
Daniel 6:20		
Psalm 7:10		
Acts 27:22, 31, 34		
Philippians 1:19		

3. Mark the following facets of salvation as *past* (as in eternity past), *present* (as in experienced in this lifetime), or *future* (as in after our resurrection):

	Past, present, or future?
Sanctification	
Election	
Glorification	
Justification	
Foreknowledge	
Regeneration	
Indwelling	
Spirit baptism	
Predestination	
Adoption	
Sealing	
Calling	

4. Which of the following statements about salvation is false:

(a) For followers of Jesus, salvation is experienced as an everlasting, unbreakable relationship with him. It has both temporal and eternal benefits.

(b) Salvation is holistic in nature, involving the spiritual as well as the physical aspects of the whole person.

(c) Jesus came to seek and save lost sinners.

(d) People were saved by works in Old Testament times, but now they are saved by grace.

(e) Because of Jesus' finished work on the cross, those who call upon the name of the Lord are saved.

5. Thinking about where we stand today as Christians, briefly describe what we *were saved* from, what we *are being saved* from now, and what we *will be saved* from in the future.

Devotional Prayer

O blessed Savior,
You knew me and loved me in eternity past.
You marked me as your own
and promised to complete your good work in me.
You descended from heaven's throne,
passed through the portals of time,
lived and died and rose again
to rescue me from sin and its curse.
You invaded the strong man's house,
bound him, and plundered his goods.
You ascended to the Father's right hand,
where you mediate on my behalf
and prepare a place for me.
You have promised to return
to set right all that's wrong
in this sinful and fallen world.
Your promise to glorify me
is as certain as your finished work at Calvary.
I bless you ...
the one who foreknew, predestined, called,
justified, and will glorify me.

— Matt. 12:29; John 14:1-3; Rom. 8:29-30;
Phil. 1:6; 1 Tim. 2:5

Article IV-A
Regeneration

Regeneration is the work of the Holy Spirit that brings a sinner from spiritual death into spiritual life.

Article IV-A of *The Baptist Faith & Message* 2000 reads:

 Regeneration, or the new birth, is a work of God's grace whereby believers become new creatures in Christ Jesus. It is a change of heart wrought by the Holy Spirit through conviction of sin, to which the sinner responds in repentance toward God and faith in the Lord Jesus Christ. Repentance and faith are inseparable experiences of grace.

Repentance is a genuine turning from sin toward God. Faith is the acceptance of Jesus Christ and commitment of the entire personality to Him as Lord and Saviour.

Comparing 1925/1963/2000

⇒ Article VII of the BF&M 1925 is titled, "Regeneration," and Article VIII is titled, "Repentance and Faith." The focus of these two articles from 1925 is captured in two paragraphs in Article IV-1: Regeneration of the BF&M 1963 and in Article IV-A: Regeneration of the 2000 edition.

⇒ Together, the 1925, 1963, and 2000 BF&Ms emphasize the Holy Spirit as the agent of regeneration, resulting in the sinner's repentance from sin and faith in the Lord Jesus Christ. Further, regeneration is a work of God's grace.

⇒ The BF&M 1963 includes two statements on justification in its article on regeneration, while both the 1925 and 2000 editions address justification separately.[1]

⇒ See Appendix 1 for a side-by-side comparison.

From Death to Life

Regeneration is the work of the Holy Spirit that brings a sinner from spiritual death into spiritual life. While Christians may disagree about such issues as the relationship between regeneration and baptism, or whether regeneration precedes faith, it is biblically faithful for a follower of Jesus to say, "I have been regenerated" or "born again."

While the Greek noun *palingenesia* appears only twice in the New Testament (Matt. 19:28; Tit. 3:5), the concept of regeneration, or new birth, is a consistent theme of Jesus and the New Testament writers. Jesus makes it clear that people must be "born again," or "born of the Spirit," if they are to see the kingdom of heaven (John 3:3, 5).

The work of the Holy Spirit, making an individual a "new creation" (2 Cor. 5:17; Gal. 6:15), prepares that person for the future work of Christ as he creates "new heavens and a new earth" (2 Pet. 3:13). All those the Spirit regenerates are assured a place with Christ when he refurbishes the cosmos, purging it completely of sin and its stain.

Regeneration is necessary because the Bible describes unbelievers as the walking dead. Not only are they spiritually dead (Eph. 2:1), but they are depicted as natural / without the Spirit (1 Cor. 2:14); blinded in their minds (2 Cor. 4:4); bound by Satan

(2 Tim. 2:26); alienated from God (Eph. 4:17-18); enemies of the Lord (Rom. 5:6-11; Col. 1:21); condemned in their unbelief (John 3:18); and in spiritual darkness (Acts 26:18; Eph. 5:8; Col. 1:13; 1 Pet. 2:9).

Regeneration is a one-time, non-repeatable act by which the Holy Spirit enters the dead human spirit of a sinner and makes him or her spiritually alive. Regeneration also is permanent. That is, a person whom God foreknows, predestines, calls, justifies, and glorifies cannot lose the gift of regeneration without losing all of the associated links in God's golden chain of redemption (see Rom. 8:29-30).

Baptismal Regeneration

Baptismal regeneration is the belief that water baptism is necessary for salvation. Proponents of this view, ranging from Roman Catholics to those in the Church of Christ, differ in their understanding of this doctrine. However, they uniformly agree that water baptism plays an essential role in obtaining everlasting life.

Supporters of this doctrine point to several passages of Scripture – for example, Mark 16:16; John 3:5; Acts 2:38; 22:16; Gal. 3:27; and 1 Pet. 3:21. These verses are more fully explored in the Missouri Baptist Convention-produced resource, *What Every Christian Should Know About Salvation.*[2] Here, we briefly provide several reasons to deny the doctrine of baptismal regeneration.

First, the Bible is clear that we are saved by grace alone, through faith alone, in Christ alone. To take away faith in Jesus as the sole requirement for salvation is universalism; to add to it is legalism (see John 1:12; 3:16; 5:24; 6:47; 20:31; Acts 4:11-12; 10:43; 13:39; 16:31; Rom. 4:4-5; Gal. 2:16; 3:6-26; Eph. 2:8-9; Tit. 3:5-7).

Second, water baptism is an important public testimony of our faith, not an essential element in our salvation. In a first-century context, for Jews embracing Jesus as Messiah, a public declaration of faith might mean banishment from family, friends, and religious leaders. Water baptism thus served as a bold and unmistakable sign of one's faith in Jesus. It demonstrated that a person was trusting fully in the finished work of Christ.

Third, the Bible says a person is condemned for not believing (John 3:18); it doesn't say a person is condemned for failing to be baptized.

Fourth, forgiveness of sins and everlasting life are received as gifts from God, by faith, apart from any works, whether considered meritorious or obedient. Water baptism symbolizes the death, burial, and resurrection of Christ, and publicly identifies the new believer with Christ.

Fifth, if water baptism is required for salvation, then no one could be saved without the help of another person, thus limiting who can be saved, and when.

Which Comes First: Faith or Regeneration?

Does faith result in regeneration, or does regeneration trigger faith? It's a question with which the Reformers wrestled.

In fully Reformed theology, regeneration precedes faith, with the Holy Spirit acting alone (*monergism*). In contrast, moderate Calvinists and Arminians contend that the Bible places faith before regeneration as the Holy Spirit works in concert with human freedom (*synergism*).

A third view, the *overcoming grace* model, falls somewhere in between. Proponents of this view argue that salvation can be monergistic (and thus all of grace), even though saving faith precedes regeneration and is a resistible gift of God. This model seeks to provide a solution to Calvinism's problem of "the well-meant offer" in which the non-elect who hear the gospel could have been saved if only God had not bypassed them. As Kenneth Keathley writes, "To offer salvation while withholding the necessary ability to respond seems like offering healing to any quadriplegic who can get up to receive it."[3]

As we wrestle with the issue, it may help to consider that regeneration and faith are, in a sense, inseparable. Whether regeneration precedes faith, or faith results in regeneration, every adopted child of God experiences both.

While the order of regeneration and faith is important, it should not divide Christians in our common fellowship, nor should it keep any of us from an obedient response to Christ's command to "Go, therefore, and make disciples of all nations" (Matt. 28:19).

Questions for Personal or Group Study

1. Among the persons of the Godhead – Father, Son, and Holy Spirit – which one serves as the agent of regeneration? What are some other terms used to describe regeneration?

2. Read Matthew 19:28 and Titus 3:5. These are the only New Testament passages employing the Greek word *palingenesia*, translated "renewal" or "regeneration." Which of these two verses applies to personal regeneration, and which applies to the future creation of new heavens and a new earth?

3. Match the following Scripture passages with the appropriate description of unbelievers:

John 3:18	Blinded in their minds
2 Corinthians 4:4	Enemies of the Lord
Ephesians 2:1	Bound by Satan
Colossians 1:21	In spiritual darkness
2 Timothy 2:26	Condemned in their unbelief
1 Peter 2:9	Dead in trespasses and sins

4. What is *baptismal regeneration*? Why do Southern Baptists reject this doctrine as unbiblical?

5. How many times may a person be regenerated by the Holy Spirit? If regeneration may be lost, what does that do to the other facets of salvation – such as foreknowledge, justification, and glorification? Refer to Romans 8:29-30.

Notes:

Devotional Prayer

Spirit of God, holy Counselor, divine Advocate:
When all seemed lost,
when I was happily descending the road to hell,
unaware and uncaring that I stood condemned,
you convicted me of my sin of unbelief,
my futile self-righteousness,
and my rightful share of Satan's judgment in hell.
You breathed new life into my once-dead human spirit,
making me a new creature in the Lord Jesus Christ.
My regeneration foretells the renewal of the earth,
when my Savior returns and makes all things new.
Thank you for sealing me, indwelling me, sanctifying me,
and serving as my down payment on my eternal home.

— Matt. 19:28; John 3:3, 7; 16:7-11; 2 Cor. 5:17; Gal.
6:15; Eph. 1:14; 1 Pet. 1:3, 23; Rev. 21:5

In justification, God *declares* us
righteous. In sanctification and
glorification ... God makes us so.

Article IV-B
Justification

Justification is the act of God declaring sinners righteous on the basis of the finished work of Christ. Believers' sins are transferred to Christ's account and exchanged for his righteousness.

Article IV-B of *The Baptist Faith & Message* 2000 reads:

" Justification is God's gracious and full acquittal upon principles of His righteousness of all sinners who repent and believe in Christ. Justification brings the believer unto a relationship of peace and favor with God.

Comparing 1925/1963/2000

⇒ Article V of the BF&M 1925 is titled, "Justification."

⇒ Two sentences on justification are included in Article IV-1: Regeneration of the BF&M 1963. These two sentences match Article IV-B: Justification of the 2000 edition.

⇒ The text on justification in the BF&M 1925 is longer than in the two more recent versions. It adds: "This blessing [justification] is bestowed, not in consideration of any works of righteousness which we have done, but through the redemption that is in and through Jesus Christ. It brings us into a state of most blessed peace and favor with God, and secures every other needed blessing."[1]

⇒ See Appendix 1 for a side-by-side comparison.

A Declaration of Righteousness

In justification, God *declares* us righteous. In sanctification and glorification, which we explore in the following chapters, God makes us so. These interlocking works of God ensure that, one day, we are fully conformed to the image of Christ.

The Greek noun *dikaiosis*, or justification, describes the act of God declaring sinners righteous on the basis of the finished work of Christ. Believing sinners are acquitted – freed of all guilt – as their sins are transferred to the account of Christ and exchanged for Christ's righteousness.

Theologians often refer to justification as *forensic*, which means "having to do with legal proceedings." This legal declaration does not change our internal character. Judges don't make defendants guilty or not guilty; they simply declare them to be one or the other.

Regeneration, indwelling, and sanctification are ways God works salvation *in* us, making us spiritually alive, taking up permanent residence in our spirits, and conforming us to the image of Christ. But justification occurs *outside* of us. Put another way, the location of justification is heaven, where God declares believing sinners in right standing before him.

The Linchpin of Salvation

In some respects, justification is the linchpin in God's great work of salvation. It is his fundamental act of blessing by which he saves us from the past and secures us for the future. Paul places justification in the golden chain of redemption in Romans 8:29-30. Those whom God foreknows, he predestines, calls, *justifies*, and glorifies.

Followers of Jesus may look backward at God's foreknowledge, election, predestination, and calling. But from the standpoint of justification, we also look forward, knowing God will complete the good work he began in us (Phil. 1:6).

Justification is grounded in Christ's death, burial, and resurrection. The apostle Paul puts it succinctly: "He was delivered up for our trespasses and raised for our justification" (Rom. 4:25). Paul further writes, "So then, as through one trespass [Adam's] there is condemnation for everyone, so also through one righteous act [Christ's] there is justification leading to life for everyone" (Rom. 5:18).

Justification is received by faith, apart from human effort (Rom. 5:1; Gal. 3:24). It is a one-time, instantaneous, non-repeatable act of God, placing us in right standing before his holy bench and ensuring that we are never subject to double jeopardy. To add works to justification, such as returning to old covenant practices that served as types and shadows of greater things to come, is to trample on the Son of God and regard as profane the blood of the new covenant (Heb. 10:29).

Justification is not to be confused with sanctification, which is the work of God setting believers apart and engaging us in a lifelong process by which we become more Christlike (1 Thess. 5:23). Justification and sanctification may be distinguished but not separated; both are divine facets of God's redemption.

The Necessity of Justification

Every person needs to be justified because every person is a sinner. Our sins place us under God's wrath. Further, no one possesses the righteousness necessary to enter the presence of God, whose eyes are too pure to look on evil (Hab. 1:13).

God the Father is the author of justification. He is the member of the Trinity who declares the believing sinner righteous. He bases this on the person and work of Christ, who, acting on behalf of helpless sinners, satisfies the claims of God's law on them.

Faith is the means by which we receive the offer of right-standing with God. Paul refers us to the case of Abraham, who "believed God, and it was credited to him for righteousness" (Rom. 4:3ff; Gal. 3:6).

Two inseparable elements come into play in justification: forgiveness and imputation. In forgiveness, God acquits us, or declares that our sins are forgiven based on the finished work of Christ. At the same time, our sins are imputed, or transferred, to the account of Christ, in exchange for his righteousness.

The results of justification are evident in the lives of believers. For example, justification brings peace with God (Rom. 5:1; Col. 1:19-20); it results in the righteousness of God (2 Cor. 5:21); it yields new attitudes and outlooks that show we are right with God and that his Spirit is working in us (Rom. 6:1-2; Tit. 2:11-14); and it produces works appropriate to the nature of the new creature that has come into being (Eph. 2:8-10).

Every human being needs God's declaration of righteousness because no one possesses the righteousness necessary to enter God's presence. Our best efforts are but filthy rags (literally, menstrual garments) in the eyes of God (Isa. 64:6).

Like the guest who arrogantly shuns the king's offer of a wedding robe, and thus is bound hand and foot and cast into outer darkness (Matt. 22:1-14); like the Pharisee who fasts and pays tithes, yet who leaves the temple unjustified (Luke 18:9-14); and like those who profess to have accomplished much in the name of Jesus, yet are told to depart as lawbreakers (Matt. 7:21-23), we cannot justify ourselves despite our most strenuous efforts.

Questions for Personal or Group Study

1. How would you describe justification in a few sentences?

2. Mark the following statements true or false:

_____ Justification is the work of God making believing sinners righteous.

_____ In justification, our sins are transferred to Christ's account and exchanged for his righteousness.

_____ While regeneration takes place *in* us, justification occurs *outside* of us; it may be said that the location of justification is heaven.

_____ We are fully and finally declared righteous when Christ raises us from the dead and glorifies us.

_____ God the Father is the author of justification.

3. What does it mean when we say justification is *forensic*?

4. Match the following Scripture passages with the appropriate result of justification:

Romans 5:1	The righteousness of God imputed to the believer
2 Corinthians 5:21	Works God has prepared from eternity past
Ephesians 2:8-10	New attitudes and outlooks
Titus 2:11-14	Peace with God

5. Why does every person need justification?

Devotional Prayer

Dearest Father, who justifies all who call on your Son,
You have declared me in right standing before your holy bench –
not because I am righteous, but because Jesus is.
Once blinded by the evil one and held captive to do his will,
once decked in the filthy rags of my own righteousness,
I now stand clothed in the righteousness of Christ,
at peace with you, bearing your name on my forehead,
free of the condemnation that banishes the guilty from your
   presence.
I honor your Son as the one delivered up for my trespasses
and raised for my justification.
It is finished – the work of redemption,
so that your declaration of my justification
is a one-time, instantaneous, non-repeatable act
that ensures I am never subject to double jeopardy.
I am forgiven; my sins are transferred
to the wounded back of your beloved Son
and marked paid in full.
In return, Christ has exchanged my sins for his righteousness.
Thank you for making me a beneficiary of your divine
   imputation.

   — Isa. 64:6; Rom. 4:25; 5:1; 8:1; 2 Cor. 4:4; 5:21; Col.
   1:19-20; 2 Tim. 2:26; Rev. 22:4

Positional sanctification is "a once-for-all event ... that transfers us from the sphere of sin to the sphere of God's holiness."

– John Frame

Article IV-C
Sanctification

Sanctification is the work of God making Christians more like Jesus.

Article IV-C of *The Baptist Faith & Message* 2000 reads:

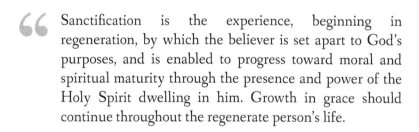 Sanctification is the experience, beginning in regeneration, by which the believer is set apart to God's purposes, and is enabled to progress toward moral and spiritual maturity through the presence and power of the Holy Spirit dwelling in him. Growth in grace should continue throughout the regenerate person's life.

Comparing 1925/1963/2000

⇒ "Sanctification" appears as Article X of the BF&M 1925.

⇒ The paragraph on sanctification in the BF&M 1963 is identical to that of the 2000 edition, with one exception: the BF&M 1963 says sanctification enables the Christian to progress toward "moral and spiritual *perfection*," echoing the BF&M 1925 language, while the 2000 version substitutes "moral and spiritual *maturity*." Likely, this update is due to changes in the English language over the years, with "perfect" once serving as a synonym for "mature." There is no suggestion Southern Baptists once believed a Christian could attain a sinless state (complete sanctification) this side of heaven.[1]

⇒ See Appendix 1 for a side-by-side comparison.

More Like Jesus

Sanctification is the work of God making Christians more like Jesus. As Millard Erickson puts it:

 Sanctification is a process by which one's moral condition is brought into conformity with one's legal status before God. It is a continuation of what was begun in regeneration, when a newness of life was conferred upon and instilled within the believer. In particular, sanctification is the Holy Spirit's applying to the life of the believer the work done by Jesus Christ.[2]

Sanctification may be understood in two ways. First, there is *positional sanctification*, the state of being separate, set apart from the common, and dedicated to a higher purpose.

The Hebrew word *qados* literally means "separate" and is used to designate particular places (like the Holy of Holies), objects (such as Aaron's garments and the Sabbath Day), and persons (especially priests and Levites).

Positional sanctification finds its place in the New Testament as a work of God occurring at the beginning of conversion. John Frame, who prefers the term *definitive sanctification*, calls this "a once-for-all event ... that transfers us from the sphere of sin to the sphere of God's holiness, from the kingdom of Satan to the kingdom of God. It is at this point that each of us joins the people of God."[3]

Second, there is *practical sanctification*, the lifelong process by which the Spirit makes us more like Jesus. This requires our ongoing submission to Christ and our obedience to the voice of the indwelling Spirit. It is the daily taking up of our cross and following Jesus (Luke 9:23).

Over the course of our Christian walk, we are conformed to Christ's character in two ways. First, the Lord implants and nurtures Christ's righteousness within us (Phil. 2:13). Second, we obey the Scriptures under the power and guidance of the Spirit so that we "grow in the grace and knowledge of our Lord and Savior Jesus Christ" (2 Pet. 3:18).

Sanctification is wholly the work of God, but it is not passive on the believer's part. The New Testament writers urge us to labor for spiritual maturity. Paul instructs us to practice virtues and avoid evil (Rom. 12:9, 16-17). We are to put to death the deeds of the body (Rom. 8:13) and present our bodies as living sacrifices (Rom. 12:1-2).

Sanctification is wholly the work of God, but it is not passive on the believer's part.

Despite the fears we may have about losing our salvation, the Spirit ensures that we persevere. Paul writes that the preaching of the cross is foolishness to those who are perishing, but "it is the power of God to us who are being saved" (1 Cor. 1:18). He uses a present participle here to convey the idea of ongoing activity.

Further, Paul tells us, "I am sure of this, that he who started a good work in you will carry it on to completion until the day of Christ Jesus" (Phil. 1:6).

Sinless Perfection?

If God's aim is to fully conform believers to the image of Christ, is it possible to attain sinless perfection within our lifetimes? The issue of *complete sanctification* has generated much disagreement throughout church history.

Generally speaking, those who answer the question in the affirmative are considered *perfectionists* and are Arminian in their doctrine, stressing human freedom and responsibility. Those who argue against perfectionism tend to be Reformed, or Calvinistic, in their doctrine, emphasizing the sovereignty of God over the free will of his creatures.

Basically, perfectionists contend that it is possible for believers to arrive at a sinless state prior to physical death. And some do, they argue. This does not mean a person *cannot* sin any longer; rather, it means he or she *does not* sin.

Going even further, it seems, are Eastern Orthodox leaders who speak of *deification* or *theosis*. This does not mean the pantheistic absorption of Christians into the person of God. Rather, it indicates that believers may acquire supernatural attributes and exercise divine energies.

Such a view goes beyond a biblical understanding of a believer's union with Christ. To partake in the divine nature does not mean sharing in exclusive attributes of God, such as eternality, omniscience, or omnipresence. Rather, it means that Christians may exhibit high levels of divine attributes such as mercy, love, and forgiveness. As Christ lives through us, we are vessels of these so-called communicable attributes, yet we never own them in the eternal, unblemished way God does.

The *non-perfectionist* view is more biblically faithful. First, sin is more subtle and pervasive than we may care to admit. Second, the Greek word translated "perfect" in Matt. 5:48 (*teleioi*) is better rendered "complete," or "mature." Finally, there is a striking absence of sinless characters in the Bible (except, of course, for Jesus). Rather than focus on earthly glorification, we should fix our eyes on Jesus, the author and finisher of our faith (Heb. 12:2 KJV).

Questions for Personal or Group Study

1. What is a simple definition of sanctification?

2. How would you describe the difference between *positional sanctification* and *practical sanctification*?

3. Match the following Scripture passages with the appropriate characteristics of sanctification:

Luke 9:23	The Lord nurturing Christ's righteousness within us
Romans 8:13	Taking up our cross and following Jesus
Romans 12:1-2	Putting to death the deeds of the body
Philippians 1:6	Presenting our bodies as living sacrifices
Philippians 2:13	Growing in grace and in the knowledge of Jesus
2 Peter 3:18	God's promise to finish the good work he began in us

4. Do you believe it's possible to attain sinless perfection in the Christian life? Why or why not?

5. What are three reasons the non-perfectionist view of sanctification is more biblically faithful than the perfectionist view?

Notes:

Devotional Prayer

O sanctifying God,
You have set me apart and marked me as your own;
the evil one has no legitimate claim to me.
You have taken up residence in the Holy of Holies – my spirit;
the usurper has been cast out and cast down.
You have transferred me into the sphere of your holiness;
Satan's kingdom is smaller and meaner as a result.
You have begun the lifelong process of making me like Jesus;
the ruler of this world buffets but cannot conquer me.
You implant and nurture Christ's righteousness in me;
Belial cannot remove it under any circumstances.
You give me the Spirit as my constant companion;
the enemy is held forever at bay.
You keep me now and forever;
sanctification leads progressively to glorification.
One day I will be like Jesus;
may I strive to be more like him today.

— Rom. 8:13; 12:1-2, 9, 16-17; 1 Cor. 1:18; Phil. 1:6;
2:13; 2 Pet. 3:18

Glorification is the means by
which God fully reverses the effects
of the Fall, purging sin and its
stain from the created order.

Article IV-D
Glorification

Glorification is the final stage in God's work of salvation. It is the crowning achievement of sanctification, in which Christians are fully conformed to the image of Christ.

Article IV-D of *The Baptist Faith & Message 2000* reads:

 Glorification is the culmination of salvation and is the final blessed and abiding state of the redeemed.

Comparing 1925/1963/2000

⇒ While the BF&M 1925 includes no article specifically devoted to glorification, Article XVI – The Resurrection ends with these words: "There will be a resurrection of the righteous and the wicked. The bodies of the righteous will conform to the glorious spiritual body of Jesus."

⇒ The paragraph on sanctification in the BF&M 2000 is identical to that of the 1963 edition.[1]

⇒ See Appendix 1 for a side-by-side comparison.

The Final Stage

Glorification is the final stage in God's work of salvation. It is the crowning achievement of sanctification, in which Christians are fully conformed to the image of Christ. It is the perfection of the body, rejoined with soul and spirit in resurrection, as well as the restoration of the universe to its original state.

Put another way, glorification is the means by which God fully reverses the effects of the Fall, purging sin and its stain from the created order. It involves the return of Jesus, the future resurrection and judgment of all people, and the creation of new heavens and a new earth.

For the most part, when Christians talk about glorification, we are referring to our future resurrection, at which time we receive incorruptible bodies similar to the body Christ had when he rose from the dead.

In this respect, Wayne Grudem provides an excellent summary statement:

 Glorification is the final step in the application of redemption. It will happen when Christ returns and raises from the dead the bodies of all believers for all time who have died, and reunites them with their souls, and changes the bodies of all believers who remain alive, thereby giving all believers at the same time perfect resurrection bodies like his own.[2]

The Meaning of Glory

We should first explore the meaning of *glory*, which translates a number of biblical words. One such word is the Hebrew *kabod*, which refers to an individual's display of splendor, wealth, and pomp. When used to describe God, however, it does not point to a singular attribute, but to the greatness of his whole nature (see Ps. 24:7-10).

In the New Testament, the Greek *doxa* carries the meaning of honor, splendor, brilliance, fame, and glory. God is the "glorious Father"

(Eph. 1:17) and the "God of glory" (Acts 7:2). In the Incarnation, Jesus bears "the glory as the one and only Son from the Father" (John 1:14).

Paul sees Christ's glorification in his ascension; Jesus is "taken up in glory" (1 Tim. 3:16). Further, the apostles preach that Christ is now exalted to the right hand of God (Acts 2:33; 5:31). And, when Jesus returns, his appearance is glorious (Tit. 2:13).

William Mounce writes:

> Because God is so glorious, it is only natural that his people want to ascribe "glory" to him. For this reason, there are many doxologies (ascriptions of glory to God) in the NT. Furthermore, every part of our lives should reflect the fact that the glorious God lives in us – even our eating and drinking.[3]

The Stages of Glorification

Scripture highlights at least four stages of glory.

First, there is glory now. As we exalt God in our lives, he begins the glorification process in us. The apostle Peter writes:

> His divine power has given us everything required for life and godliness through the knowledge of him who called us by his own glory and goodness. By these he has given us very great and precious promises, so that through them *you may share in the divine nature*, escaping the corruption that is in the world because of evil desire (2 Pet. 1:3-4, emphasis added).

Peter does not mean that believers become little gods or that we acquire the unique qualities of deity such as eternality, omnipotence, omniscience, and omnipresence. Rather, he seems to be saying that we participate in God's moral excellence and one day are morally perfected.

Second, there is glory in death. When we breathe our last, followers of Jesus leave our earthly bodies behind. Our souls and spirits pass into the presence of God in heaven, where we glorify God in ways previously unknown as he endows us with moral and spiritual perfection.

Third, there is glory in resurrection. Full glorification for followers of Jesus takes place when he calls our bodies from the grave and gives us incorruptible bodies similar to the body he bore when he rose from the dead. Read more about the glorification of our bodies in the next chapter.

Finally, there is glory in restoration. Jesus refers to this as "the renewal of all things, when the Son of Man sits on his glorious throne" (Matt. 19:28). Peter urges us to wait for "new heavens and a new earth, where righteousness dwells" (2 Pet. 3:13). And in John's vision of the world to come, he sees "a new heaven and a new earth" (Rev. 21:1).

For now, Christians are not promised an earthly walk in the park, but an arduous race through enemy territory. If we're living faithfully, we may expect hardship, shunning, persecution, and pain – not health, riches, fame, and ease.

Christ is not the means to an end; he is the end himself, accessed through a narrow gate (Matt. 7:13) and pursued down a path of good works he laid out for us ahead of time (Eph. 2:10). He walks with us, however, urging our faithfulness to him while we "go through many hardships to enter the kingdom of God" (Acts 14:22).

In the end, we may rejoice with the apostle Paul that "the sufferings of this present time are not worth comparing with the glory that is going to be revealed to us" (Rom. 8:18).

Questions for Personal or Group Study

1. Why do we say glorification is the final stage of God's work of salvation?

2. What does the word *glory* mean as it's used in the Old Testament (Heb. *kabod*) and New Testament (Gr. *doxa*)?

3. Match the following stages of glory to their proper descriptions:

Glory now	Our souls and spirits pass into the presence of Christ in heaven.
Glory in death	We participate in God's moral excellence.
Glory in resurrection	Jesus creates new heavens and a new earth.
Glory in restoration	Our physical bodies are raised in the likeness of Christ's glorified body.

4. Mark the following statements true or false:

_____ In glorification, God fully reverses the effects of the Fall.

_____ The Hebrew word *kabod* and the Greek term *doxa* refer only to human glory.

_____ When Jesus returns, his glory will be concealed.

_____ Glorification applies to Christians' future state, as well as to the future restoration of the earth.

_____ After our resurrection, we become little gods in our glorified state.

5. Read Romans 8:18-30. How does Paul contrast the present state of our bodies with our future state? How does he compare the fallen world in which we now live with the world to come?

Devotional Prayer

Dearest glorified Son,
seated at the Father's right hand,
resplendent in the brilliant light of the seven fiery torches,
holding the keys of death and Hades ...
I am foreknown, elected, predestined,
called, regenerated, justified,
indwelt, sealed, and sanctified.
All of this I owe to you and your redemptive work
with the Father and the Holy Spirit.
But I am not yet glorified,
not yet fully conformed to your image,
not yet able to live under the complete control
of your Spirit in a restored Eden.
Yet I praise you and worship you,
for you most certainly will finish the work
of purging sin and its stain from my whole being.
You will set things right in me
and in the fallen world you reclaimed
when you suffered, died, and rose again.
May I live each day in joyous anticipation
of your return in glory
and for my glorification.
Come, Lord Jesus!

— *Phil. 1:6; Rom. 8:29-30; Heb. 12:2; Rev. 1:18; 4:5;*
22:20

"In the resurrection the believer will have a Spirit-constituted physical body. The brokenness and decay of the old body will be gone."

– Kenneth Bailey

Article IV-D (Continued)
Our Glorified Bodies

Physical resurrection is the apogee of personal glorification, for in it we shrug off the last vestiges of sin that have clung to our mortal bodies. In glorification, the effects of the Fall are fully and finally reversed.

Article IV-D of *The Baptist Faith & Message* 2000 reads:

 Glorification is the culmination of salvation and is the final blessed and abiding state of the redeemed.

Comparing 1925/1963/2000

⇒ While the BF&M 1925 includes no article specifically devoted to glorification, Article XVI – The Resurrection ends with these words: "There will be a resurrection of the righteous and the wicked. The bodies of the righteous will conform to the glorious spiritual body of Jesus."

⇒ The paragraph on sanctification in the BF&M 2000 is identical to that of the 1963 edition.[1]

⇒ See Appendix 1 for a side-by-side comparison.

The Final Stage

As we learned in the last chapter, glorification is the means by which God fully reverses the effects of the Fall, purging sin and its stain from the created order. It involves the return of Jesus, the future resurrection and judgment of all people, and the creation of new heavens and a new earth.

The glory we experience now as Christ lives in us, and the glory we experience in death as our souls / spirits ascend into heaven, are partial works of glorification. But full glorification for followers of Jesus takes place when he calls our bodies from the grave and gives us incorruptible bodies similar to the body he bore when he rose from the dead.

Physical resurrection is the apogee of personal glorification, for in it we shrug off the last vestiges of sin that have clung to our mortal bodies. In glorification, the effects of the Fall are fully and finally reversed.

At the return of Christ, all who have died in the Lord are resurrected. Their souls / spirits – their immaterial essence in heaven with Jesus – are reunited with their bodies, resulting in complete personal glorification. The body, soul, and spirit are fully conformed to the image of Christ and thus free of any effects of the Fall.

Christians alive on the earth at the return of Christ are instantly transformed as they are given glorified bodies. At the same time, their souls / spirits are perfected as well.

Prepared for Glory

While several New Testament passages describe this transformation, Paul gives us the most complete picture in 1 Corinthians 15. In verses 35-41, he uses three analogies from nature – seeds, flesh, and celestial bodies – to explain how God takes the bodies of deceased believers and prepares them for everlasting glory.

With that as a backdrop, Paul distinguishes believers' mortal bodies from their immortal ones. Their bodies therefore are:

Sown in corruption, raised in incorruption (v. 42). Physical death is the natural result of living in a perishable body. We get sick, grow old, and simply wear out. Even death by natural causes means the fittest body can't live forever. Even those raised from the dead in Scripture – from the son of the widow at Zarephath to Lazarus – died a second time because they did not receive glorified bodies.

However, God fashions our resurrection bodies in such a way that they are immune to sickness, disease, aging, and decay. Put another way, our glorified bodies are guaranteed to last as long as Jesus' resurrected body endures (forever).

Sown in dishonor, raised in glory (v. 43). Paul may be thinking ahead to verses 47-49 in depicting our earthly bodies as dishonorable. The first man, Adam, left us a legacy of dishonor. He willfully disobeyed God, made excuses for his sin, and even implicated God in the process. As a result, he bequeathed to us a natural tendency to live independently of God, which manifests itself in sin and shame in every human life.

Our earthly rap sheets are exceedingly long and disgraceful. Standing in sharp contrast, however, are believers' resurrection bodies, which no longer bear the stamp of sin, and thus radiate the Christlike qualities of holiness, integrity, reliability, and wisdom.

Sown in weakness, raised in power (v. 43). The Greek word rendered "weakness" is *astheneia* and means frailty, sickness, or disease. Our present earthly bodies cannot overpower the effects of living in a sinful and fallen world. Ultimately, the curse of sin is victorious even over the most fit human specimens, and we all succumb to death in a thousand awful ways.

But our resurrection bodies are raised in power. The Greek *dynamis* means might, strength, or ability. Often in the New Testament, it is connected with miraculous power, particularly with respect to the power of God and the miracles of Jesus. Our glorified bodies are powered by God, who destroys the vestiges of sin clinging to our earthly bodies.

Sown a natural body, raised a spiritual body (v. 44). Paul distinguishes between the bodies we now possess and the bodies we put on in glorification. Today, we have a *soma psychikos*, or natural body. This means more than just flesh and blood, however. It refers to a living human being that belongs to the natural world.

But in resurrection, we receive a *soma pneumatikos*, or "spiritual body." This means the Holy Spirit preserves and directs our glorified bodies. This does not imply that our glorified bodies are ghostly, ethereal, non-material figures, for that casts doubt on Christ's physical resurrection from the dead and his promise to ultimately make us like him.

As Kenneth Bailey explains:

 In the resurrection the believer will have a Spirit-constituted physical body. The brokenness and decay of the old body will be gone. The new body will be a physical body like the resurrected body of Christ. Such a truly glorious vision and promise calls for an exuberant hymn of victory.[2]

Our glorification in resurrection is not a lengthy process. Rather, Paul reveals to us a mystery: "We will not all fall asleep, but we will all be changed, in a moment, in the twinkling of an eye, at the last trumpet" (vv. 51-52).

Whether we are raised from the dead or transformed as living Christians on earth into glorified believers, the promise of Christ's return should cause us to rejoice, as Paul does: "But thanks be to God, who gives us the victory through our Lord Jesus Christ!" (v. 57).

Questions for Personal or Group Study

1. For Christians, what is the connection between physical resurrection and glorification?

2. Where does the immaterial part of a Christian – that is, his or her soul / spirit – reside between physical death and glorification?

3. Which of the following analogies from nature does Paul *not* use in 1 Corinthians 15 to explain how God takes the bodies of deceased believers and prepares them for everlasting glory:

    (a) Seeds
    (b) Water
    (c) Flesh
    (d) Clouds
    (e) Celestial bodies

4. Match the following statements about our bodies in death to their appropriate contrasts with our bodies in glorification:

Sown in corruption ...	Raised in power
Sown in dishonor ...	Raised a spiritual body
Sown in weakness ...	Raised in incorruption
Sown a natural body ...	Raised in glory

5. How would you compare and contrast the *spiritual bodies* we're going to receive in glorification with the *natural bodies* we possess today?

Notes:

Devotional Prayer

Father, Son, and Holy Spirit,
co-equal, co-eternal authors of my salvation ...
I look for the day when the Father says all is ready,
the bridal chamber is finished,
the banquet table is set.
I look for the day when the Son returns in glory
to claim his bride and live forever with her
in unspeakable joy and unbroken intimacy.
I look for the day when the Spirit completely
empowers and controls my new body.
At death, I know that my body is sown in corruption;
but at Jesus' return, it is raised in incorruption.
At death, my body is sown in dishonor;
but at Jesus' return, it is raised in glory.
At death, my body is sown in weakness;
but at Jesus' return, it is raised in power.
At death, my body is sown a natural body –
that is, a body belonging to this world;
but at Jesus' return, it is raised a spiritual body –
a body the Spirit preserves and directs.
My salvation is secure in Christ
and is almost complete.
As I walk this vale of sorrow, may I hold to your promise
that one day you will wipe the very tears from my eyes
with your nail-scarred hands,
and banish death, grief, crying, and pain
from the new heavens and earth,
as former things that have passed away.

— Matt. 22:1-14; 25:1-13; 1 Cor. 15:42-49; Rev. 19:6-9; 21:4

Every Christian should readily acknowledge that the Bible teaches divine election. Disagreements arise with respect to how this doctrine is biblically defined, and how it's applied.

Article V

God's Purpose of Grace

God's work of salvation, from foreknowledge in eternity past to glorification in eternity future, displays his goodness, wisdom, and holiness. It further shows that his divine sovereignty is consistent with human free will.

Article V of *The Baptist Faith & Message* 2000 reads:

 Election is the gracious purpose of God, according to which He regenerates, justifies, sanctifies, and glorifies sinners. It is consistent with the free agency of man, and comprehends all the means in connection with the end. It is the glorious display of God's sovereign goodness, and is infinitely wise, holy, and unchangeable. It excludes boasting and promotes humility.

All true believers endure to the end. Those whom God has accepted in Christ, and sanctified by His Spirit, will never fall away from the state of grace, but shall persevere to the end. Believers may fall into sin through neglect and temptation, whereby they grieve the Spirit, impair their graces and comforts, and bring reproach on the cause of Christ and temporal judgments on themselves; yet they shall be kept by the power of God through faith unto salvation.

Comparing 1925/1963/2000

⇒ The first paragraph of the BF&M 1963 and the first paragraph of the BF&M 2000 read similarly to the full text of the 1925 edition.

⇒ Both the BF&M 1963 and 2000 add a second paragraph, which reads nearly the same word-for-word in both editions.

⇒ The BF&M 1925 adds Article XI – Perseverance, which addresses God's work of keeping believers secure. This reads similarly to the second paragraph of Article V of the 1963 and 2000 editions.[1]

⇒ See Appendix 1 for a side-by-side comparison.

Divine Election

Every Christian should readily acknowledge that the Bible teaches divine election. Disagreements arise with respect to how this doctrine is biblically defined, and how it's applied.

The word *election* in Scripture is derived from the Greek *eklegomai*, which means "to choose something for oneself." The Bible also uses words such as "choose," "predestine," "foreordain," and "call" to indicate that God has entered into a special relationship with certain individuals and groups through whom he has decided to fulfill his purposes.

As the BF&M 2000 statement above implies, election is God's choice of certain individuals to salvation before the foundation of the world. The Reformed (Calvinist) position on election is that it is *unconditional*; that is, God selected specific persons for everlasting life based solely on his divine will and good pleasure, not on foreseen faith. In other words, God foreknows all future events – including responses to the gospel message – because he first ordained them.

The Arminian position is that God's election is *conditional*; that is, God selected specific persons for salvation based on foreseeing their belief and repentance in response to the gospel message. As taught by Jacobus Arminius, after whom Arminianism is named, God's election to salvation is the election of *believers*, which means that election is conditioned on faith. Arminius also insisted that God's foreknowledge of people's choices did not cause those choices or make them necessary.

Between Calvinism and Arminianism is Molinism. Named for Luis Molina, a sixteenth-century Jesuit priest, Molinism argues that God perfectly accomplishes his will in free creatures through the use of his omniscience. Molinism seeks to reconcile two biblical truths: (1) God exercises sovereign control over all his creation, and (2) human beings make free choices for which they must give an account.

As Kenneth Keathley explains, "Molinism simultaneously holds to a Calvinistic view of a comprehensive divine sovereignty and to a version of free will (called *libertarianism*) generally associated with Arminianism."[2] Put another way, Molinism borrows a high view of God's sovereignty from Calvinism and a high view of human freedom from Arminianism.

Some theologians hold to a fourth view: God's election is *corporate*; that is, according to Ephesians 1:4-6, God chose believers *in Christ* before the foundation of the world. Jesus is the "elect one," and the church consists of people who freely choose to receive Christ.

What is Reprobation?

Reprobation is a term that describes those who are left in their sinful and fallen states and thus are eternally damned.

Generally, those who embrace Reformed theology argue that reprobation is *unconditional*, meaning that God's decree of damnation for certain people results in their unbelief.

Those who hold a more moderate view of Reformed theology, as well as Arminians, contend for *conditional* reprobation. This means God foresees the unbelief of certain individuals and thereby decrees their damnation. However, as with the Arminian view of election, God's foreknowledge doesn't cause their unbelief, or make it necessary.

Thus, election and reprobation essentially are two sides of the same coin:

- Election is gracious and eternal; reprobation is just and eternal.
- Election is established in Christ; reprobation is declared by Christ.
- Election is conditioned on faith and repentance; reprobation is conditioned on unbelief and rebellion.
- Election is personal in its application; so is reprobation.

The doctrine of election, and the related doctrines of foreknowledge and predestination, continue to serve as flashpoints among Christian fellowships. That's disheartening, because there is a great deal of common ground to be shared.

While followers of Jesus may debate whether election is conditional or unconditional, we all agree that God is the author of salvation. He is sovereign, free, gracious, and just. He withholds salvation from no one and banishes no one to hell without that person's consent. And he entrusts his highest created beings with an ability to make decisions for which he holds them accountable.[3]

Questions for Personal or Group Study

1. How would you explain the similarities and differences between *unconditional election* and *conditional election*? Which of these concepts appears most biblically faithful to you?

2. Besides unconditional election and conditional election, what are two other positions on the doctrine of divine election?

3. Which of the following is a correct definition of *reprobation*:

   (a) The condition of those left in their sinful and fallen states, who thus are eternally damned

   (b) The promise of a second chance for salvation after physical death and prior to resurrection and final judgment

   (c) A description of the sin nature in all people

   (d) A synonym for predestination

   (e) A description of life in hell, where unbelievers are destined to revisit their sins throughout all eternity

4. Match the following statements about election and reprobation:

Election is gracious and eternal ...	Reprobation is personal in its application
Election is established in Christ ...	Reprobation is conditioned on unbelief and rebellion
Election is conditioned on faith and repentance ...	Reprobation is declared by Christ
Election is personal in its application ...	Reprobation is just and eternal

5. Why do you think the doctrine of divine election is so hotly debated among Christians today? Where can we find common ground?

Devotional Prayer

Holy Trinity,
All praise to thee for electing me to salvation,
by foreknowledge of God the Father,
through sanctification of the Spirit,
unto obedience and sprinkling of the blood of Jesus;
I adore the wonders of thy condescending love,
marvel at the true believer's high privilege
within whom all heaven comes to dwell,
abiding in God and God in him ...
Continue to teach me that Christ's righteousness
satisfies justice and evidences thy love;
Help me to make use of it by faith
as the ground of my peace
and of thy favour and acceptance,
so that I may live always near the cross.[4]

Membership in the universal church
cannot be bought, begged, stolen,
inherited, earned, or conferred by any
human or angelic being. It comes only by
the grace of God through faith in Jesus.

Article VI
The Church

The church is neither a physical structure nor a man-made institution. It is the living, breathing body of Christ spoken of in two ways in Scripture: as a local body of believers, and as the universal body of the redeemed under the Lordship of Jesus.

Article VI of *The Baptist Faith & Message* 2000 reads:

> A New Testament church of the Lord Jesus Christ is an autonomous local congregation of baptized believers, associated by covenant in the faith and fellowship of the gospel; observing the two ordinances of Christ, governed by His laws, exercising the gifts, rights, and privileges invested in them by His Word, and seeking to extend the gospel to the ends of the earth. Each congregation operates under the Lordship of Christ through democratic processes. In such a congregation each member is responsible and accountable to Christ as Lord. Its scriptural officers are pastors and deacons. While both men and women are gifted for service in the church, the office of pastor is limited to men as qualified by Scripture.

The New Testament speaks also of the church as the Body of Christ which includes all of the redeemed of all the ages, believers from every tribe, and tongue, and people, and nation.

Comparing 1925/1963/2000

⇒ Article XII in the BF&M 1925 is titled "The Gospel Church." It corresponds to Article VI in the 1963 and 2000 versions.

⇒ Article VI of the BF&M 2000 is longer than the 1963 version, and even longer than the 1925 edition. The first (lengthy) sentence of the BF&M 2000 reads similarly to the first paragraph of the BF&M 1963 and to the entire Article XII of the 1925 edition.

⇒ The 1963 and 2000 versions make it clear the local church is an "autonomous" body operating under "democratic processes." While the BF&M 1925 does not directly address this, it does not contradict later editions.

⇒ All three editions affirm pastors and deacons as scriptural officers of the local church, although the BF&M 1925 uses the terms "bishops, or elders, and deacons."

⇒ Finally, both the 1963 and 2000 versions add a final paragraph acknowledging the universal church as the body of Christ, including the redeemed of all the ages.[1]

⇒ See Appendix 1 for a side-by-side comparison.

Called Out Ones

The Greek word translated "church" is *ekklesia* and means "called out ones." The term appears more than one hundred times in the New

Testament and refers to the community of believers over which Jesus is head (Col. 1:18). Thus, the church is neither a physical structure nor a man-made institution. It is the living, breathing body of Christ.

The Bible generally speaks of the church in two significant ways: as *universal* and *local*.

The universal church is the complete body of believers who have trusted in Jesus as Lord and Savior. It cannot be divided along denominational lines, although such distinctions provide clarity in beliefs and practices.

Membership in the universal church cannot be bought, begged, stolen, inherited, earned, or conferred by any human or angelic being. It comes only by the grace of God through faith in Jesus (John 1:12; 5:24; Eph. 2:8-9).

Key passages that address the universal church include Matt. 16:18; 1 Cor. 15:9; Eph. 1:22-23; 5:29-30; Col. 1:18; and Rev. 5:9-10; 7:9. For example, Jesus tells his disciples he will build his church in such a way that the gates of Hades will not overpower it (Matt. 16:18). Paul confesses to being a former persecutor of the church (1 Cor. 15:9). And the apostle John sees a vast multitude of redeemed people from every nation, tribe, and language standing before the throne in heaven (Rev. 7:9).

However, most New Testament references to the church focus on local congregations. The local church may be defined as a body of baptized believers in Jesus who live in the same community and gather at a common place for worship, fellowship, instruction, and service.

Scripture instructs Christians to identify with a local church in order to grow spiritually (Heb. 10:24-25). It is through the local church that believers exercise their spiritual gifts and take part in worship, fellowship, Bible study, church discipline, missions, and other communal activities.

Key passages that address the local church include Acts 9:31; Rom. 16:5; 1 Cor. 1:2; 16:19; and Col. 4:15. For example, after Saul's conversion, Luke records that the church throughout all Judea, Galilee, and Samaria has peace and is strengthened (Acts 9:31). No doubt, this is a reference to local congregations of the universal church.

Body, Building, Bride

The New Testament describes the church in many ways:

First, as a *body*, with Christ as the head and believers as various parts of the body (1 Cor. 12:12-31). Paul writes that Jesus is "the head of the body, the church" (Col. 1:18).

Second, as a *building*, with Christ as the chief cornerstone, the teaching of the apostles as the foundation, and believers as the building stones (Matt. 16:13-18; 21:42; 1 Cor. 3:11; Eph. 2:19-22; 1 Pet. 2:1-11). Peter writes that followers of Jesus are "living stones, a spiritual house ... being built to be a holy priesthood to offer spiritual sacrifices acceptable to God through Jesus Christ" (1 Pet. 2:5).

Third, as a *bride*, to be kept pure and eager for the coming of the bridegroom, Jesus Christ (Matt. 25:1-13; Mark 2:19-20; John 3:29; 2 Cor. 11:2). Jesus' parable of the ten virgins illustrates the bridegroom-bride relationship between Christ and his church. In addition, Jesus stresses the necessity that Christians remain pure and be ready for his return (Matt. 25:1-13).

Fourth, as a *mystery*, hidden from Old Testament believers but revealed to the apostles and given to Christians. The mystery of the church is closely tied to the mystery of salvation through Jesus, which welcomes Jews and Gentiles as adopted sons and daughters of God (Eph. 3:1-12; 5:32; Rev. 10:7). In his instructions to husbands and wives, who are united as one flesh, Peter declares, "This mystery is profound, but I am talking about Christ and the church" (Eph. 5:32).

Finally, as an *organization* with officers and ordinances.

Officers and Ordinances

Ephesians 4:11-15 tells us Christ gave to the church *apostles*, referring to the twelve, but also apparently referring in a general sense to messengers sent on errands from one church to another (2 Cor. 8:23; Phil. 2:25), and in a general sense to all believers who help spread the gospel (John 17:18; 20:21).

Christ also gave the church *prophets*, or public proclaimers of God's word; *evangelists*; *pastors*; and *teachers*. Apostles, prophets, and evangelists tend to serve the universal church, while pastors and teachers do their work mainly in the context of the local church.

For the local church, the officers are *pastors* and *deacons*. New Testament words that Baptists identify with the pastoral office include terms translated as *bishop, elder,* and *pastor.*[2] These are complementary terms that add to our understanding of the pastor's role and responsibilities.

Bishop means overseer – that is, someone who superintends the work of others in the local church. *Elder* refers to one who counsels with maturity, dignity, and wisdom. And *pastor* describes a shepherd who loves and cares for those God has entrusted to his service (Acts 20:28; Phil. 1:1; 1 Tim. 3:1-7; Tit. 1:6-9).

Deacons serve the local church in ways that enable pastors to devote themselves to teaching the word of God and prayer (Acts 6:3-6). The scriptural qualifications for pastors and deacons are featured in 1 Timothy 3:1-13 and Titus 1:6-9.

The two ordinances of the church are baptism and the Lord's Supper, which we explore in the next chapter.

What Makes a Local Church?

Finally, there are several key distinctives of the local church: (1) autonomy, meaning that every local congregation has the authority to fulfill its ministry; (2) the lordship of Jesus over the church; (3) a congregation of believers who covenant together to fulfill the Great Commission; (4) a common baptism that binds us together as believers and establishes the boundaries of membership in the congregation; and (5) voluntary cooperation with other like-minded believers.

In Southern Baptist life, voluntary cooperation is best exhibited through a local church's affiliation with an association, a state convention, and the Southern Baptist Convention. It's also demonstrated through voluntary giving to state, national, and international causes through the Cooperative Program (see Appendix II: Missouri Baptists and the Cooperative Program).

Questions for Personal or Group Study

1. What is the difference between the universal church and the local church?

2. Look up the following passages of Scripture and mark whether the reference is to the universal church or the local church?

	Universal or local church?
Matthew 16:18	
Acts 9:31	
1 Corinthians 1:2	
Ephesians 1:22-23	
Colossians 1:18	
Colossians 4:15	
Revelation 7:9	

3. List and briefly explain five ways the New Testament describes the church.

4. Match the following church leaders with their appropriate descriptions:

Apostles	Public proclaimers of God's word
Prophets	Servants in the local church, enabling pastors to focus on the word of God and prayer
Evangelists	Those specially gifted to win souls
Pastors	Primarily the twelve, but also messengers sent from one church to another
Teachers	Those specially gifted to train others in the local church
Deacons	Overseers, wise counselors, and shepherds in the local church

5. List five key distinctives of the local church.

Devotional Prayer

Dearest Lord Jesus,
our great high priest, mediator, and intercessor ...
We are your called-out ones,
and we owe to you our membership in God's household,
built on the foundation of the apostles and prophets,
with you as the chief cornerstone.
Make us grow into a holy temple in the Lord.
Fit us together into a building for God's dwelling in the Spirit.
You are the head of the church, and we are the body.
You are the cornerstone, and we are the bricks.
You are the bridegroom, and we are your cherished bride.
You are our peace, and we are to be peacemakers.
May we walk worthy of the calling we have received,
with all humility, gentleness, and patience,
bearing with one another in love,
making every effort to keep the unity of the Spirit
through the bond of peace.

— Rom. 8:34; 2 Cor. 11:2; Eph. 2:19-22; 4:1-3; 1 Tim.
2:5; Heb. 4:14-15

Article VII
Baptism and the Lord's Supper

Southern Baptists refer to baptism and the Lord's Supper as ordinances, meaning the Lord commands believers to carry out these symbolic activities, which picture the finished work of Christ and prepare us for his imminent return.

Article VII of *The Baptist Faith & Message* 2000 reads:

 Christian baptism is the immersion of a believer in water in the name of the Father, the Son, and the Holy Spirit. It is an act of obedience symbolizing the believer's faith in a crucified, buried, and risen Saviour, the believer's death to sin, the burial of the old life, and the resurrection to walk in newness of life in Christ Jesus. It is a testimony to his faith in the final resurrection of the dead. Being a church ordinance, it is prerequisite to the privileges of church membership and to the Lord's Supper.

The Lord's Supper is a symbolic act of obedience whereby members of the church, through partaking of the bread and the fruit of the vine, memorialize the death of the Redeemer and anticipate His second coming.[1]

Comparing 1925/1963/2000

⇒ Article XIII of the BF&M 1925 ("Baptism and the Lord's Supper") corresponds to Article VII of the 1963 and 2000 editions.

⇒ Article VII of the BF&M 1963 and Article VII of the BF&M 2000 read identically.

⇒ The 1925 edition refers to the "bread and wine" of the Lord's Supper, while the more recent editions use "bread and the fruit of the vine."

⇒ See Appendix 1 for a side-by-side comparison.

Ordinances of the Church

Southern Baptists refer to baptism and the Lord's Supper as *ordinances*. That means the Lord commands believers to carry out these symbolic activities, which picture the finished work of Christ and prepare us for his imminent return.

Ordinances have no saving value, for a person receives everlasting life only by faith in Jesus. Even so, baptism and the Lord's Supper are important acts of obedience.

Some, like Roman Catholics, refer to baptism and Holy Communion as *sacraments*, meaning they are necessary for salvation.

Others, like Presbyterians, also call baptism and the Lord's Supper *sacraments*, but that doesn't mean they are necessary for salvation. Rather, they are "means of God's grace" – special ways God speaks to our hearts, gives us a visible way of establishing the difference between believers and unbelievers, and prepares us to serve him.

Baptism by Immersion

Baptism is the *immersion* of a believer in water. The Greek word for *baptize* means "to dip in or under," "immerse," or "submerge." Greeks used this term to signify the dying of a garment, or the drawing of wine by dipping a cup into a bowl.[2]

Scriptural baptism follows *justification* – the work of God declaring a believing sinner to be in right standing before him.

Believers are to be immersed rather than sprinkled or poured over with water because immersion properly pictures: (1) our identification with the crucified, buried, and risen Savior; (2) the death of our old life, and the resurrection to new life in Christ; (3) baptism by the Holy Spirit into the body of Christ, which took place at conversion (Rom. 8:9; 1 Cor. 12:13); and (4) our faith in the future resurrection of the dead.

As believers, we are baptized because Jesus commands us to be baptized (Matt. 28:19-20) and instructs us to follow him (Matt. 16:24). Further, we may take comfort in at least two biblical truths.

First, *Jesus was baptized*, identifying him as the Son of God and initiating a new epoch in God's plan of redemption as the Spirit descended on him (Matt. 3:15-17). Therefore, we are identified with the person and work of Jesus when we follow him in baptism.

Second, *the early Christians were gladly baptized* as a testimony of their faith. For example, on the Day of Pentecost, three thousand new believers followed Peter's call to be baptized (Acts 2:41; see also Acts 8:36-38; 10:47-48; 16:30-33).

The Lord's Supper

Also known as *communion*, the Lord's Supper is a symbolic act of obedience through which believers memorialize the death of Jesus and anticipate his return. This is done by eating bread and drinking the fruit of the vine – the bread symbolizing Christ's broken body, and the drink symbolizing his shed blood at Calvary (Matt. 26:17-30; Mark 14:22-26; Luke 22:19-20; 1 Cor. 10:16; 11:23-30).

Jesus institutes the Lord's Supper on the night of his betrayal and arrest as he celebrates Passover with his apostles. Passover is a remembrance of what God did in delivering the Israelites from Egyptian bondage (see Exod. 12:1-28). At that time, God was going to carry out the last of ten plagues, striking dead every first-born male – man and beast – throughout Egypt.

But the death angel passed over the homes of believing Israelites who sprinkled the blood of a lamb over their door posts.

Now, Jesus, the Lamb of God, establishes a similar memorial for a new covenant:

 And he took bread, gave thanks, broke it, gave it to them, and said, "This is my body, which is given for you. Do this in remembrance of me." In the same way he also took the cup after supper and said, "This cup is the new covenant in my blood, which is poured out for you" (Luke 22:19-20).

Only believers may take part in the Lord's Supper. Jesus instructs those who partake to "Do this in remembrance of me" (1 Cor. 11:24). Unbelievers have no reason to remember Christ's sacrificial death, since they've rejected him. And since they have not entered into a covenant relationship with Christ, they have no hope of drinking the fruit of the vine with him in his kingdom.

Christians living in rebellion against God should abstain from the Lord's Supper until their sins are confessed and repentance takes place. The apostle Paul makes it clear that a Christian should "examine himself" (1 Cor. 11:28) before partaking of the Lord's Supper. Failure to do so invites the chastening of God (1 Cor. 11:29-30).

The Bible gives no instruction as to the frequency with which the Lord's Supper should be observed. Some churches observe the Lord's Supper every Sunday; others, once or twice a month, or quarterly. Paul simply told us that "as often as you eat this bread and drink the cup, you proclaim the Lord's death until he comes" (Cor. 11:26).

Questions for Personal or Group Study

1. What's the difference between an *ordinance* and a *sacrament*?

2. Briefly share four reasons believers are to be immersed rather than sprinkled or poured over with water in baptism?

3. What are two biblical truths that should encourage new believers in Jesus to be baptized?

4. Look up the following passages of Scripture and match them with the appropriate truth about the Lord's Supper:

Exodus 12:1-28	Jesus institutes the Lord's Supper during the Passover celebration.
Luke 22:14-20	The unleavened bread symbolizes the body of Jesus, which is broken for us.
1 Corinthians 11:24	Believers should carefully examine themselves before taking part in the Lord's Supper.
1 Corinthians 11:25	The Lord's Supper is tied to Passover, a remembrance of God's deliverance of the Israelites from Egyptian bondage.
1 Corinthians 11:26	We proclaim the Lord's death until he returns every time we partake of the Lord's Supper.
1 Corinthians 11:27-32	The cup symbolizes the new covenant Jesus establishes through his spilled blood on the cross.

5. Does your church have a process for preparing new believers for baptism, such as a required new members' class or pastoral counseling? If so, why is that important? Also, how often does your church observe the Lord's Supper? Why has it chosen that frequency?

Devotional Prayer

O Son of Man, Lord of the Sabbath,
conqueror of Satan, sin, and death ...
We are blood-bought sinners,
beneficiaries of your ransom at Calvary,
once dead in trespasses and sins
but now alive for as long as you live.
We embrace your finished work
as we submit obediently to water baptism,
by which also we anticipate our future glorification.
We memorialize your sacrificial and substitutionary death –
the breaking of your body and the shedding of your blood –
as we partake of bread and cup in the Lord's Supper.
These symbols of your humble life
and glorious victory over the grave
stand as ordinances of the church –
acts of obedience that help us remember
the days of your passion
and enable us to eagerly anticipate
your future return in glory.
As new believers, we are immersed in water
in the name of the Father, Son, and Holy Spirit.
As redeemed followers of Jesus,
we take the bread and cup in remembrance of you.

> *— Matt. 12:8; 26:26-30; 28:19-20; John 14:19; Acts*
> *8:36-38; 10:47-48; 16:30-33; 1 Cor. 11:23-26*

The designation of Sunday as the
Lord's Day is rooted in Scripture
and in Christian tradition dating
back to the days of the apostles.

Article VIII

The Lord's Day

*The earliest Christians shifted their day of observance from
Saturday to Sunday because Christ appeared to his disciples
on the first day of the week.*

Article VIII of *The Baptist Faith & Message* 2000 reads:

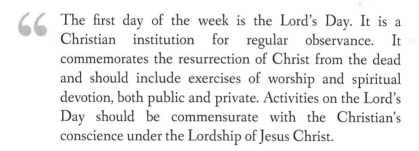 The first day of the week is the Lord's Day. It is a
Christian institution for regular observance. It
commemorates the resurrection of Christ from the dead
and should include exercises of worship and spiritual
devotion, both public and private. Activities on the Lord's
Day should be commensurate with the Christian's
conscience under the Lordship of Jesus Christ.

Comparing 1925/1963/2000

⇒ Article XIV in the BF&M 1925 is titled "The Lord's Day"
and corresponds to Article VIII in the 1963 and 2000 editions.

⇒ Article XIV in the BF&M 1925 and Article VIII in the
BF&M 1963 read identically and urge Southern Baptists to

observe the Lord's day "by refraining from worldly amusements, and resting from secular employments, work of necessity and mercy only being excepted."

⇒ The 2000 edition replaces the statement above with: "Activities on the Lord's Day should be commensurate with the Christian's conscience under the Lordship of Jesus Christ."[1]

⇒ See Appendix 1 for a side-by-side comparison.

Sunday as the Lord's Day

The designation of Sunday as the Lord's Day is rooted in Scripture and in Christian tradition dating back to the days of the apostles. For example, Luke records that the apostle Paul and the disciples gathered in Troas for the breaking of bread and preaching on "the first day of the week" (Acts 20:7).

However, since a Jewish day begins at sundown, worship in Troas took place on Saturday night as Westerners reckon time. It helps us empathize with the sleepy-headed Eutychus, who wearied of Paul's preaching and fell to his death from a third-story window, necessitating a miracle to restore his life (Acts 20:8-12).

Elsewhere in the New Testament, we see followers of Jesus gather for worship on the first day of the week, which came to be known as the Lord's Day (1 Cor. 16:2; Rev. 1:10). For Israelites, this could be any time from sundown on Saturday to sundown on Sunday.

No doubt, worship began to shift from the Sabbath (Saturday) to the first day of the week in commemoration of Christ's resurrection. The resurrected Jesus appears to his disciples on the evening of the first day of the week (John 20:19). The celebration of Christ's victory over Satan, sin, and death on that day became the hallmark of Christian worship, but not immediately.

As David Schrock points out:

 It's worth remembering how easily we can superimpose our church traditions on Scripture. We do well to learn what the early church actually practiced. In the earliest days, worship consisted of Sabbath-keeping and resurrection-celebrating on two different days. In time, the former decreased and the latter persisted.[2]

In his book, *A Brief History of Sunday: From the New Testament to the New Creation*, Justo Gonzalez lists three theological reasons for worship on Sunday.

First, Sunday observance of the Lord's Day points to the centrality of the resurrection in the Christian faith. As Paul wrote to the Corinthians: "For I passed on to you as most important what I also received: that Christ died for our sins according to the Scriptures, that he was buried, that he was raised on the third day according to the Scriptures ...." (1 Cor. 15:3-4).

Second, Sunday is the first day of a new creation. As Paul identifies believers as new creations in Christ (2 Cor. 5:17), so the first day after the Sabbath would, according to Genesis, have been a day of new creation.

Third, Sunday is the "eighth day," a day related both to circumcision and also "the final day of eternal rest and joy."[3]

Gonzalez also points out that the Lord's Day was not universally observed as a "day of rest" until Constantine initiated the practice of Sabbath-keeping on Sunday in the fourth century.[4]

Christians have debated – and continue to debate – the proper day for corporate worship. The Fourth Commandment is clear: "Remember the Sabbath day, to keep it holy" (Exod. 20:8). Jewish people have considered Saturday the Sabbath from Old Testament times. This raises an important question: Is the Sabbath the Lord's Day?

Some groups, such as Seventh-Day Adventists, believe Christians should gather on the last day of the week – Saturday – in keeping with the Old Testament command. In their view, the church should follow the pattern of the Jewish people.

But as Charles Kelley and others point out in their 2007 study of *The Baptist Faith & Message*, this understanding raises at least two problems. The first is biblical: "We have ample reason to believe that the earliest Christians shifted their day of observance from Saturday to Sunday because Christ appeared to His disciples on the first day of the week."

The second problem with interpreting the Lord's Day as Saturday is the practice and tradition of the church, writes Kelley: "It is absolutely clear that from the earliest days of the church, Christians gathered on Sunday rather than on Saturday."[5]

Additional debates arise over acceptable activities on the Lord's Day. This goes all the way back to the time of Jesus and the apostles, when the Jewish authorities heaped so many man-made restrictions on people that the Sabbath became a burden. Jesus addresses this when he tells the religious leaders, "The Sabbath was made for man and not man for the Sabbath" (Mark 2:27).

In a similar way, Christians today – with good intentions – may be tempted to twist the Lord's Day into acts of legalism. This misses the point of the Lord's Day, which is to be a day of joy and peace.

Certainly, Christians should order their lives so that the priority of the Lord's Day is corporate worship. This involves songs and hymns, Scripture reading, prayer, and the study of God's word (Col. 3:16). It also includes private acts of devotion such as Bible reading, prayer, and deeds of Christian service (2 Cor. 8:1-3; 1 Thess. 5:12, 17; 2 Tim. 3:16; Jas 1:27).

Last, whether one engages in corporate worship on Saturday, Sunday, or another day of the week, the focus should be on celebrating the finished work of the resurrected Christ. The specific day devoted to worship may be one of the "disputed matters" Paul addresses in Romans 14.

Questions for Personal or Group Study

1. Mark the following statements true or false:

_____ The Lord's Day was, and is, and always will be Saturday.

_____ The designation of Sunday as the Lord's Day is rooted in Scripture and in Christian tradition dating back to the days of the apostles.

_____ Worship began to shift from the Sabbath (Saturday) to the first day of the week after Constantine ordered it to be so.

_____ Sunday observance of the Lord's Day points to the centrality of the resurrection in the Christian faith.

_____ No true Christian would skip church on Sunday to attend a Kansas City Chiefs football game.

2. Read John 20:19. On what day of the week does Jesus appear to his disciples? How might this have influenced the church's gathering for worship on a certain day of the week?

3. What three theological reasons does Justo Gonzalez offer for worshiping on Sunday?

4. Do you think worshiping on Sunday violates the Fourth Commandment? Why or why not?

5. How should we treat those who insist that Saturday (the Sabbath) is the Lord's Day?

Notes:

Devotional Prayer

O Lord my Lord,
This is thy day,
the heavenly ordinance of rest,
the open door of worship,
the record of Jesus' resurrection,
the seal of the sabbath to come,
the day when saints militant and triumphant
unite in endless song....
Give me in rich abundance
the blessings the Lord's Day was designed to impart;
May my heart be fast bound against worldly
thoughts or cares;
Flood my mind with peace beyond understanding;
may my meditations be sweet,
my acts of worship life, liberty, joy,
my drink the streams that flow from thy throne,
my food the precious Word,
my defense the shield of faith,
and may my heart be more knit to Jesus.[6]

"The primary meaning of both the Hebrew word *malkuth* in the Old Testament and of *basileia* in the New Testament is the rank, authority and sovereignty exercised by a king."

– *George Ladd*

Article IX
The Kingdom

The kingdom is God's reign, his authority to rule.

Article IX of *The Baptist Faith & Message* 2000 reads:

> The Kingdom of God includes both His general sovereignty over the universe and His particular kingship over men who willfully acknowledge Him as King. Particularly the Kingdom is the realm of salvation into which men enter by trustful, childlike commitment to Jesus Christ. Christians ought to pray and to labor that the Kingdom may come and God's will be done on earth. The full consummation of the Kingdom awaits the return of Jesus Christ and the end of this age.

Comparing 1925/1963/2000

⇒ Article XXV in the BF&M 1925 is titled "The Kingdom" and corresponds to Article IX in the 1963 and 2000 editions.

⇒ Article IX of the BF&M 1963 and Article IX of the BF&M

2000 read identically, except that the word *kingdom* is
capitalized in the more recent edition.

⇒ The BF&M 1925 reads quite differently from later editions,
particularly in its definition of the kingdom. Compare the first
two sentences of the 2000 version above with the following
sentence from the BF&M 1925: "The Kingdom of God is the
reign of God in the heart and life of the individual in every
human relationship, and in every form and institution of
organized human society."

⇒ The BF&M 1925 also differs from later versions in its
description of the consummation of the kingdom, although all
three editions point to the return of Christ as the defining
event.[1]

⇒ See Appendix 1 for a side-by-side comparison.

God's Authority to Rule

The terms *kingdom of God, kingdom of heaven,* and *kingdom* (with
reference to the kingdom of God / heaven) appear nearly 150 times in
Scripture. None of these passages offers a straightforward definition of
the kingdom. Yet the kingdom is proclaimed throughout the Old
Testament and is the primary focus of Jesus' teaching.

Many of Jesus' parables tell us what the kingdom is like. The
apostles preach the gospel of the kingdom – the good news of
redemption and restoration received through faith in Jesus Christ. And
biblical prophecies of the last days point toward a time when God's
kingdom comes in its fullness.

So, what is the kingdom of God? Simply stated, the kingdom is
God's reign, his authority to rule.

As George Ladd notes:

  The primary meaning of both the Hebrew word *malkuth*
in the Old Testament and of *basileia* in the New

Testament is the rank, authority and sovereignty exercised by a king. A *basileia* may indeed be a realm over which a sovereign exercises authority; and it may be the people who belong to that realm and over whom authority is exercised; but these are secondary and derived meanings. First of all, a kingdom is the authority to rule, the sovereignty of the king.[2]

Creation, Fall, Redemption, Restoration

Perhaps the kingdom of God is best understood in light of the biblical account of creation, fall, redemption, and restoration.

God created everything and declared it "very good indeed" (Gen. 1:31). Initially, all creatures in the invisible and visible realms served their creator faithfully. There was peace throughout God's kingdom.

But Satan led an angelic rebellion against the Lord and his authority. Then, under the influence of the evil one, Adam fell, and a competing kingdom rose up in opposition to God – a kingdom over which Satan reigns.

In reply, God promised a virgin-born redeemer who would crush the serpent's head (Gen. 3:15). The Old Testament expanded this view with roughly four hundred prophecies and foreshadows of a coming Messiah. When the Son of God came to earth, he essentially invaded Satan's rebel kingdom.

Jesus' sinless life, death, burial, and resurrection brought salvation to sinful humans. And his promised return one day will completely reverse the effects of the Fall and restore the created order to its pristine perfection.

The Kingdom in the Old and New Testaments

In the Old Testament, the kingdom is revealed as God's rule over creation. The writers depict God as a king whose sovereignty extends to the ends of the earth (Ps. 47:2, 7; 95:3-5). This means the Lord orchestrates the rise and fall of nations (2 Chron. 20:6; Job 12:23; Ps. 22:28). Further, benevolence and justice characterize his rule (Ps. 99:4).

The Old Testament writers understand that God's purposes would be worked out in the unfolding of human history. Even so, the Old Testament picture of the kingdom of God is incomplete, pointing to the works of the coming Messiah.[3]

In the New Testament, Jesus preaches about the kingdom and tells parables to reveal what it's like. Early in his ministry, he declares that the kingdom "has come near" (Matt. 4:17), meaning that where Jesus is present, the kingdom of God is present. His miracles – turning water into wine, calming the seas, raising the dead, and casting out demons – validate his authority to rule. Further, they provide a window into the future, when the kingdom in its fullness is void of death, grief, crying, and pain (Rev. 21:4).

The Mystery of the Kingdom

Finally, it's important to understand the *mystery* of the kingdom of God, which Jesus addresses in his parables (Matt. 13:11). The Greek *mysteria* means what we can know only by divine revelation. This has particular value in helping us understand the already / not yet quality of the kingdom. That is, some aspects of the kingdom are to be experienced in the present, while others await future fulfillment.

First-century Jews were looking for a political and military kingdom based on their understanding of the Hebrew Scriptures. They largely ignored the prophecies in Isaiah 53 and elsewhere of a Suffering Servant and thereby rejected Jesus, who declared that his kingdom "is not of this world" (John 18:36).

So, the mystery of the kingdom is that it must first come without fanfare in the Lamb of God who takes away the sin of the world (John 1:29). The kingdom is present where Jesus is present – on the earth briefly two thousand years ago, and today in the hearts of believers. One day, the kingdom comes in fullness as the Lion of Judah returns to claim his throne, judge all people, cast the usurper (Satan) and his followers into the lake of fire, and create new heavens and a new earth (2 Pet. 3:10-13; Rev. 19:11-16; 21-22).

As we await the full revealing of the kingdom, Christians should pray, as the apostle John prayed, "Come, Lord Jesus!" (Rev. 22:20).

Questions for Personal or Group Study

1. How would you briefly define the kingdom of God? What does the biblical concept of the kingdom mean for the universe in general, and for followers of Jesus in particular?

2. Match the following phases of the kingdom with their appropriate descriptions:

Creation	Jesus invades Satan's kingdom and starts rescuing the evil one's captives.
Fall	God creates everything and declares it "very good indeed."
Redemption	Jesus returns and creates new heavens and a new earth.
Restoration	Satan rebels, Adam follows his lead, and a competing kingdom arises.

3. Mark the following statements true or false:

_____ In the Old Testament, the kingdom is revealed as God's rule over creation.

_____ Jesus' miracles – turning water into wine, calming the seas, raising the dead, and casting out demons – validate his authority to rule.

_____ Satan rules a rebel kingdom today and will continue to rule it in hell.

_____ The vast majority of first-century Israelites believed the kingdom of God came in its fullness with the preaching of John the Baptist.

_____ There is an already / not yet quality to the kingdom of God.

4. Read Matthew 12:22-32. What evidence does Jesus offer the religious leaders to show that the kingdom of God is present among them (v. 28)? Who is the strong man in Jesus' parable (v. 29)? Why will the religious leaders not be forgiven of their blasphemy?

5. What is the *mystery* of the kingdom of God?

Devotional Prayer

O righteous sovereign,
King of kings and Lord of lords,
You rule in holiness, grace, and divine justice.
The earth and everything in it are yours,
for you laid the foundations of the world on the seas,
and established it on the rivers.
You, and only you, are to be worshiped as King.
Your kingdom is not of this present, evil world system,
but it came to earth in the person of Jesus,
and it will be established in fullness when he returns.
The mystery of your kingdom is its now / not yet character;
Christ reigns in our hearts today,
and soon he reigns over a new earth from the throne of David.
The evil one feigns authority,
but you invaded his treasonous kingdom
and daily plunder his goods.
You have prepared a place for the usurper;
one day he and his traitorous comrades will be banished there.
You also have prepared a place for us, your citizens;
one day you will take us there to be with you forever.
May your kingdom – your authority to rule – come,
and may your will be done
on earth as it is in heaven.

— Ps. 24:1-2; Matt. 6:10; 12:28-29; 25:41; John 14:1-3;
18:36; Rev. 20:10

Heaven is the temporary home of
believers. The restored earth is our
eternal home and God's throne.

Article X
Last Things

The world as we know it ends with the return of Jesus, but it's not really the end of the world, for Christ creates new heavens and a new earth.

Article X of *The Baptist Faith & Message* 2000 reads:

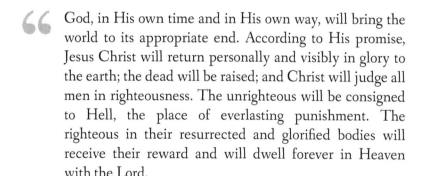 God, in His own time and in His own way, will bring the world to its appropriate end. According to His promise, Jesus Christ will return personally and visibly in glory to the earth; the dead will be raised; and Christ will judge all men in righteousness. The unrighteous will be consigned to Hell, the place of everlasting punishment. The righteous in their resurrected and glorified bodies will receive their reward and will dwell forever in Heaven with the Lord.

Comparing 1925/1963/2000

⇒ The BF&M 1925 addresses *last things* in three articles: Article XV – The Righteous and the Wicked; Article XVI – The Resurrection; and Article XVII – The Return of the Lord.

The content of these three articles corresponds with the text of Article X of the 1963 and 2000 editions but goes into more detail.

⇒ Article X of the BF&M 1963 and Article X of the BF&M 2000 read identically, except for differences in the capitalization of *hell / heaven* (1963) and *Hell / Heaven* (2000).

⇒ Article XVII of the BF&M 1925 ends with this exhortation: "It is the duty of all believers to live in readiness for his coming and by diligence in good works to make manifest to all men the reality and power of their hope in Christ."[1]

⇒ See Appendix 1 for a side-by-side comparison.

How the World Ends

Contemporary culture embraces the drama of a cataclysmic end of the world as we know it. In the 1979 film *Mad Max*, a shortage of fossil fuels drives the breakdown of society, prompting leather-clad hoodlums in bizarre vehicles to terrorize anyone with a full tank of gas.

In *Planet of the Apes*, astronaut George Taylor discovers he has traveled through space and time, returning to an earth where humans are mute and loud-mouthed armor-wearing primates are in charge.

And in Ray Bradbury's short story, "August 2026: There Will Come Soft Rains," a robotic house continues to serve its human tenants long after they have become burnt silhouettes on the wall, presumably the victims of a nuclear holocaust.

Whether entertaining or horrifying, the end of the world is a topic of great interest and much debate. World religions and cults often contrive detailed apocalyptic views, including specific dates that, when missed, leave their leaders red-faced and their followers asking neighbors to return the cookware they thought they would never need again.

Christians have reliable information about the end of days through God's revelation in Scripture. And while we may vigorously debate the order of events surrounding the return of Christ, we can all agree on seven biblical truths about how the world ends.

First, the world ends when the Father says so. Jesus makes this clear in his prophecies and parables. He tells his followers, "Now concerning that day and hour no one knows – neither the angels of heaven, nor the Son – except the Father alone" (Matt. 24:36).

First-century Jews hearing Jesus' parable of the ten virgins understand that no wedding begins until the father declares everything ready. Meanwhile, like the bridesmaids waiting for the groom, we are exhorted to "be alert, because you don't know either the day or the hour" (Matt. 25:13).

Second, the world ends with the return of Jesus. It's important to look for Jesus' physical and visible appearing, in which angelic and human followers accompany him in glory as he takes his rightful place on the throne of David and restores all things.

Jesus promises, "I will come again," and he makes it clear that people witness his return with their own eyes (John 14:1-3). For example, the Lord tells his followers, "For as the lightning comes from the east and flashes as far as the west, so will be the coming of the Son of Man" (Matt. 24:27). He further states that "all the peoples of the earth ... will see the Son of Man coming on the clouds of heaven with power and great glory" (Matt. 24:30).

Remember also what the angels tell the apostles at Jesus' ascension: "This same Jesus, who has been taken from you into heaven, will come in the same way that you have seen him going into heaven" (Acts 1:11).

Third, the world ends with the resurrection of the dead. Christians are divided as to whether all people are raised from the dead at the same time, or whether there are multiple resurrections stretching across a thousand years or more. In any case, we should heed the plain teaching of Jesus that "a time is coming when all who are in the graves will hear his [the Son of Man's] voice and come out" – either to the resurrection of life or the resurrection of condemnation (John 5:28-29).

Fourth, the world ends with judgment. Jesus tells us in Revelation 22:12, "Look, I am coming soon, and my reward is with me to repay each person according to his work." Resurrected believers face judgment for their stewardship – that is, for their degree of obedience or disobedience to God's commands – and are rewarded for faithful stewardship (Matt. 16:27; Luke 14:13-14; Rom. 14:10-12; 1 Cor. 3:11-15; 2 Cor. 5:10).

Resurrected unbelievers also stand before Christ and are punished in varying degrees for their evil deeds. All are cast into the lake of fire (Rev. 20:11-15). There is a day of reckoning for those who reject Christ and persecute his people (Rom. 12:19; 2 Thess. 1:6-10; Heb. 10:29-31; Rev. 19:11-21).

Fifth, the world ends with separation – specifically a separation of God's people from those who have rejected Christ. Jesus promises his followers, "I will come again and take you to myself, so that where I am you may be also" (John 14:3). The wicked, however, are cast into hell, which Jesus describes as "outer darkness" (Matt. 8:12) and "the blazing furnace" (Matt. 13:42, 50), a terrifying depiction of eternity far away from the light of the world (John 8:12).

Sixth, the world ends with the creation of new heavens and a new earth. The apostle Paul describes the present world in which we live as "groaning together with labor pains" beneath the weight of sin (Rom. 8:22). But a day is coming when the returning Christ purges our fallen world of sin and its stain – a fiery refinement that results in a pure, fully restored creation (2 Pet. 3:10-13). Revelation 21-22 provides further details of the new heavens and new earth.

Seventh, the world ends as it began, with God dwelling with us. Heaven is the temporary home of believers. The restored earth is our eternal home and God's throne. The apostle John hears a loud voice from God's throne declaring, "Look, God's dwelling is with humanity, and he will live with them. They will be his peoples, and God himself with be with them and be their God" (Rev. 21:3).

In the next verse, we're told that God wipes away every tear from our eyes. Death is no more, neither are grief, crying, and pain. These are "the previous things that have passed away" (Rev. 21:4).

The curse of sin is gone. Satan, evil spirits, and rebellious humans are banished. Eden – the intersection of the unseen realm God inhabits and the physical world he created – is restored.

"Amen! Come, Lord Jesus!" (Rev. 22:20).

Questions for Personal or Group Study

1. Why do you think there's so much interest in the end of the world?

2. What's your favorite apocalyptic book, movie, or television series? Who's the villain? The hero? What's the threat to mankind? And how does the story end? Finally, how does this futuristic tale compare with the biblical account of the last days?

3. Match the following Scripture passages to their corresponding truths about the end of the world:

Matthew 24:36	The world ends with the resurrection of the dead.
John 5:28-29	The world ends with judgment.
2 Peter 3:10-13	The world ends with the creation of new heavens and a new earth.
Revelation 21:3	The world ends when the Father says so.
Revelation 22:12	The world ends as it began, with God dwelling with us.

4. Mark the following statements true or false:

_____ All Christians agree about the exact order of events surrounding the return of Jesus.

_____ Jesus was being less than completely honest when he said he didn't know the day and hour of his return.

_____ One day, every person is physically resurrected and stands in final judgment before Christ.

_____ Heaven is the temporary home of departed Christians; ultimately, God has destined us to live with him on a recreated earth.

_____ The words of Jesus about hell are meant to scare us into good behavior, but we shouldn't worry; a loving God would never send anyone there.

5. Read Revelation 21:1-4. What's missing from the new heavens and new earth?

Devotional Prayer

Blessed Jesus,
who sits at the Father's right hand,
enthroned in glory,
possessing all authority in heaven and on earth ...
We wait expectantly for your return.
You are coming as a thief in the night;
as a bridegroom at midnight;
with the voice of the archangel
and the trumpet of God;
in the company of your holy ones;
to gather your elect from the four winds;
to resurrect and judge all people;
to bring your reward as well as your wrath;
to banish the evil one and his followers;
to reward your faithful servants;
to create new heavens and a new earth;
to wipe all tears from our eyes.
We are weary of this sinful and fallen world.
We welcome the Day of the Lord.
And we rejoice in your promise to make all things new.

— Matt. 24:31; 25:1-13; 28:18; 1 Thess. 4:16; 5:2;
2 Pet. 3:10-13; Jude 14; Rev. 16:15; 21:5; 22:12

"Those who have received the gospel are to share it. This obligation God placed upon redeemed men, not upon angels. If men do not tell the story, it will not be told."

— *Herschel Hobbs*

Article XI
Evangelism and Missions

Evangelism is sharing the gospel with the goal of leading others to repentance and faith in Jesus. Missions may be defined as the church's responsibility to bring God's love and the Christian gospel to all people through evangelism, education, and ministry.

Article XI of *The Baptist Faith & Message* 2000 reads:

 It is the duty and privilege of every follower of Christ and of every church of the Lord Jesus Christ to endeavor to make disciples of all nations. The new birth of man's spirit by God's Holy Spirit means the birth of love for others. Missionary effort on the part of all rests thus upon a spiritual necessity of the regenerate life, and is expressly and repeatedly commanded in the teachings of Christ. The Lord Jesus Christ has commanded the preaching of the gospel to all nations. It is the duty of every child of God to seek constantly to win the lost to Christ by verbal witness undergirded by a Christian lifestyle, and by other methods in harmony with the gospel of Christ.

Comparing 1925/1963/2000

⇒ Article XXIII of the BF&M 1925 is titled "Evangelism and Missions." It corresponds with Article XI in the 1963 and 2000 editions and reads roughly the same.

⇒ The 1963 and 2000 versions of this article are very close in verbiage, except the BF&M 2000 inserts, "The Lord Jesus Christ has commanded the preaching of the gospel to all nations."

⇒ Further, the BF&M 2000 departs from the previous versions in one other way. The 1925 and 1963 editions read: "It is the duty of every child of God to seek constantly to win the lost to Christ *by personal effort* ...." The BF&M 2000 reads, "It is the duty of every child of God to seek constantly to win the lost to Christ *by verbal witness undergirded by a Christian lifestyle* ...." (italics added).[1]

⇒ See Appendix 1 for a side-by-side comparison.

Make Disciples of All Nations

Evangelism and missions are the duties and privileges of every Christian in obedience to the command of Jesus to make disciples of all nations (Matt. 28:18-20). They are grounded in the authority of Jesus, and they find their source in the heart of God, who loves all people and desires them to repent and believe the good news (John 3:16; 2 Pet. 3:9).

Simply stated, evangelism is sharing the gospel with the goal of leading others to repentance and faith in Jesus. The word *evangelism* comes from the Greek noun *euaggelion* (a good message) and the verb *euaggelizo* (to announce, declare, or preach this good news).

Notice that the Greek word for angel – *aggelos* – is tucked inside *euaggelion*. An angel in Scripture is a messenger, sometimes heaven-sent and sometimes human. As Jessica Brodie writes, "Those who practice evangelism are indeed delivering a message: One of extraordinarily good news, life-giving and transformative, with eternal ramifications."[2]

In Matthew 28:1-7, the Lord sends an angel to roll away the stone from Jesus' tomb – not so Jesus may get out, but so the first eyewitnesses of his resurrection may see the empty grave. The angel tells the women:

> Don't be afraid, because I know you are looking for Jesus who was crucified. He is not here. For he has risen, just as he said. Come and see the place where he lay. Then go quickly and tell his disciples, "He has risen from the dead and indeed he is going ahead of you to Galilee; you will see him there ..." (vv. 5-7).

These are the last recorded words of the angel on that day. He has fulfilled his mission. From that time forward, redeemed people bear the responsibility to proclaim the good news.

As Herschel Hobbs notes, "Those who have received the gospel are to share it. This obligation God placed upon redeemed men, not upon angels. If men do not tell the story, it will not be told."[3]

It should be remembered that the gospel is an exclusive message – and a nonnegotiable one – that deliverance from sin and its consequences is found only in Jesus, who is the way, the truth, and the life (John 14:6; cf. Acts 4:12). We should share this good news graciously, never resorting to coercion, violence, or any other means that denies Christ's free offer of salvation and the Holy Spirit's work of conviction (John 16:7-11).

Reaching the Nations

Missions may be defined as the church's responsibility to bring God's love and the Christian gospel to all people through evangelism, education, and ministry.

As Charles Kelley, Richard Land, and Albert Mohler point out, "Evangelism and missions go hand in hand, but missions has historically been understood as a means of reaching nations and people groups rather than individuals alone."[4]

After his resurrection, Jesus gives many missionary commands to his followers (e.g., John 20:21-23; Acts 1:8). In the Great Commission, he specifically tells them to "make disciples of all nations," a command that necessarily involves global missions (Matt. 28:18-20). The apostles obey, taking the good news out from Jerusalem to Judea, Samaria, and the ends of the earth (Acts 1:8).

Christ's command is not just to the apostles and other eyewitnesses of his resurrection. By extension, it is a command to all believers and to his church.

Hobbs writes that church history is instructive regarding the power of the gospel. The church in Jerusalem resisted the call to evangelize the nations, while the church at Antioch embraced it (Acts 13:1-3). Hobbs further notes that the times of greatest spiritual death throughout the church age are times when evangelism and missions are at their lowest ebb. In contrast, the times of greatest spiritual power have come "when the tides of evangelism and missions have been at their highest level."[5]

Evangelism and missions are not the responsibilities of religious professionals alone. They are the privileges of every Christian, and they carry a great promise. As we spread the good news, we may rest assured the Lord is fulfilling his promise to Abraham to bless all people through the Messiah (Gen. 12:1-3; 18:18; Acts 3:24-26).

The apostle John, in his vision of heaven from the island of Patmos, records:

> After this I looked, and there was a vast multitude from *every nation, tribe, people, and language,* which no one could number, standing before the throne and before the Lamb. They were clothed in white robes with palm branches in their hands. And they cried out in a loud voice: Salvation belongs to our God, who is seated on the throne, and to the Lamb! (Rev. 7:9-10, emphasis added).

Questions for Personal or Group Study

1. What's a simple definition of *evangelism*? A simple definition of *missions*? How are evangelism and missions related to each other?

2. What's the significance of the fact that the Greek word for angel (*aggelos*) is imbedded in the Greek word for evangelism (*euaggelion*)?

3. Why is it important to keep in mind that the Christian gospel is an exclusive message – a message that deliverance from sin and its consequences is found only in Jesus?

4. Mark the following statements true or false:

_____ Christ has entrusted the gospel to redeemed humans, not angels.

_____ Coercion, and sometimes even violence, are legitimate means of proclaiming the gospel; it's the result that matters.

_____ Evangelism and missions go hand in hand.

_____ Evangelism and missions are primarily the duties of professional ministers like pastors and missionaries.

_____ Through evangelism and missions, God is fulfilling his promise to Abraham to bless all nations through the Messiah.

_____ In the apostle John's vision of heaven, recorded in the Book of Revelation, Jesus makes it clear that only 144,000 are saved.

5. Read John 16:7-11. How does Jesus describe the role of the Holy Spirit in bringing lost sinners to faith in Christ?

Devotional Prayer

O Lord,
I bless thee that the issue of the battle
between thyself and Satan
has never been uncertain,
and will end in victory.
Calvary broke the dragon's head,
and I contend with a vanquished foe,
who with all his subtlety and strength
has already been overcome.
When I feel the serpent at my heel
may I remember him whose heel was bruised,
but who, when bruised, broke the devil's head....
O thou whose every promise is balm,
every touch life,
draw near to thy weary warrior,
refresh me, that I may rise again
to wage the strife,
and never tire until my enemy is trodden down.[6]

It's good for us to study the arts and
sciences, because in them we see
the beauty, magnitude, divine
wisdom, and glory of the creator.

Article XII
Education

All truth is God's truth. Therefore, education must be grounded in what God has revealed to us. We are to embrace truth, teach it to our children, model it in our lives, proclaim it in our churches, and share it with the world.

Article XII of *The Baptist Faith & Message* 2000 reads:

> Christianity is the faith of enlightenment and intelligence. In Jesus Christ abide all the treasures of wisdom and knowledge. All sound learning is, therefore, a part of our Christian heritage. The new birth opens all human faculties and creates a thirst for knowledge. Moreover, the cause of education in the Kingdom of Christ is co-ordinate with the causes of missions and general benevolence, and should receive along with these the liberal support of the churches. An adequate system of Christian education is necessary to a complete spiritual program for Christ's people.
>
> In Christian education there should be a proper balance between academic freedom and academic responsibility. Freedom in any orderly relationship of

human life is always limited and never absolute. The
freedom of a teacher in a Christian school, college, or
seminary is limited by the pre-eminence of Jesus Christ,
by the authoritative nature of the Scriptures, and by the
distinct purpose for which the school exists.

Comparing 1925/1963/2000

⇒ Article XX of the BF&M 1925 is titled "Education." It
corresponds with Article XII in the 1963 and 2000 editions but
is more concise.

⇒ Article XX of the BF&M 1925 reads much like the first
paragraph of the 2000 edition. The first paragraph of the BF&M
1963, however, only mirrors the last half of the first paragraph in
the 2000 version.

⇒ The 1963 and 2000 versions of Article XII add an identical
second paragraph that goes into some detail about the balance
between academic freedom and academic responsibility for
Christian educators.[1]

⇒ See Appendix 1 for a side-by-side comparison.

How God Reveals Himself

God's word instructs us to pursue knowledge and wisdom. And since all
truth is God's truth, education must be grounded in what God has
revealed to us. We are to embrace truth, teach it to our children, model it
in our lives, proclaim it in our churches, and share it with the world.

God has revealed himself to us in at least four significant ways.

First, God has revealed himself in creation. "The heavens declare the
glory of God," writes the psalmist, "and the expanse proclaims the work
of his hands" (Ps. 19:1).

The apostle Paul adds that the unbelieving world stands condemned
for rejecting God's self-revelation in the physical realm: "For his

invisible attributes, that is, his eternal power and divine nature, have been clearly seen since the creation of the world, being understood through what he has made. As a result, people are without excuse" (Rom. 1:20).

It's good for us to study the arts and sciences because in them we see the beauty, magnitude, divine wisdom, and glory of the creator. Christians, above all, should promote and pursue the revealed truths of God accessible through the lenses of telescopes and microscopes.

Second, God has revealed himself in conscience. Paul writes that unbelieving Gentiles "show that the work of the law is written on their hearts. Their consciences confirm this. Their competing thoughts either accuse or even excuse them on the day when God judges what people have kept secret" (Rom. 2:15-16).

In other words, moral absolutes are gifts of God, designed to point people to the divine lawgiver.

Third, God has revealed himself in Christ. He is "the radiance of God's glory and the exact expression of his nature" (Heb. 1:3). Jesus is the eternal Son of God, who humbled himself by adding sinless humanity to his deity (see Phil. 2:5-11). He could truthfully tell Philip, "The one who has seen me has seen the Father" (John 14:9). Further, as God, Jesus not only knows the truth; he *is* the truth (John 14:6).

Finally, God has revealed himself in the canon of Scripture, which was breathed out by God and given to us for "teaching, for rebuking, for correcting, for training in righteousness, so that the man of God may be complete, equipped for every good work" (2 Tim. 3:16-17).

Tethered to Biblical Truth

The Bible says parents have the primary responsibility for educating their children in the faith. This means taking advantage of every opportunity to teach God's words "when you sit in your house and when you walk along the road, when you lie down and when you get up. Bind them as a sign on your hand and let them be a symbol on your forehead. Write them on the doorposts of your house and on your city gates" (Deut. 6:7-9).

Local churches should follow Christ's charge to "make disciples of all nations ... teaching them to observe everything I have commanded you" (Matt. 28:19-20). Followers of Jesus are to dwell on everything true, honorable, just, and pure (Phil. 4:8-9). Christian education undergirds evangelism and missions. Therefore, local churches should organize comprehensive teaching and training ministries.

On a broader scale, Southern Baptists cooperate at the associational, state, and national levels to advance Christian education. Depending on how members of 47,000 autonomous Southern Baptist churches choose to cooperate, this may encompass six theological seminaries, dozens of colleges and universities, and even private Christian schools and homeschooling networks. Together, Southern Baptists are united in the belief that the goal of Christian education is to know God and make him known.

This is not to say that secular, public education is inherently evil. Quite the contrary. However, we must remember that education of any kind not tethered to biblical truth ultimately drifts into error.

In Christian education, we should strive for a balance between academic freedom and academic responsibility, understanding that academic freedom is not a license for Christian teachers to promote unbiblical doctrines.

As Charles Kelley, Richard Land, and Albert Mohler point out, "Southern Baptists must expect professors at our institutions to teach in accordance with and not contrary to *The Baptist Faith & Message*, to defend the faith rather than to subvert it, and to inculcate in the next generation a reverent and mature understanding of Christian truth."[2]

Christians should love the Lord with all our minds (Matt. 22:37). This requires us to steep our thoughts in God's word and submit ourselves to its truth as the standard by which all philosophies, ideas, and truth claims are to be judged (John 17:17; 2 Tim. 2:15).

Questions for Personal or Group Study

1. Since all truth is God's truth, how should followers of Jesus handle the truth with respect to education?

2. Match the following Scripture passages to their corresponding method of God's self-revelation:

Psalm 19:1	God reveals himself in the person of Christ.
John 14:9	God reveals himself in creation.
Romans 2:15-16	God reveals himself in the canon of Scripture.
2 Timothy 3:16-17	God reveals himself in conscience.

3. Read Deuteronomy 6:7-9. What does this passage tell us about teaching God's word in our homes?

4. How do Southern Baptists promote Christian education at the church, state convention, and national convention levels?

5. Mark the following statements true or false:

_____ The Bible prohibits Christians from sending their children to public schools or secular universities.

_____ All truth is God's truth.

_____ Christian education undergirds evangelism and missions.

_____ God has revealed himself in creation, conscience, Christ, and all religious writings.

_____ In Christian education, we should strive for a balance between academic freedom and academic responsibility.

_____ Southern Baptists cooperate at the associational, state, and national levels to promote Christian education.

Notes:

Devotional Prayer

Omniscient Lord,
All truth is your truth,
and apart from your revelation
we are in darkness.
We bless you that you have revealed yourself
to us in creation,
for the heavens declare your glory;
in conscience,
for you have written your law on our hearts;
in Christ,
for he is the radiance of your glory
and the exact expression of your nature;
and in the canon of Scripture,
for you have breathed it out and given it to us
for teaching, rebuking, correcting, and training in righteousness.
May we love you with all our minds,
steep our thoughts in your word,
and submit ourselves to its truth
as the standard by which we judge all claims of truth.

— Ps. 19:1; Matt. 22:37; John 17:17; Rom. 1:20; 2:15-
16; 2 Tim. 2:15; 3:16-17; Heb. 1:3

The very idea of stewardship may be
traced to the garden of Eden, where
God commands Adam and Eve,
"Be fruitful, multiply, fill the earth,
and subdue it" (Gen. 1:28).

Article XIII
Stewardship

Stewardship is not ownership. Good stewards faithfully manage what belongs to someone else and readily understand they are accountable to the owner.

Article XIII of *The Baptist Faith & Message* 2000 reads:

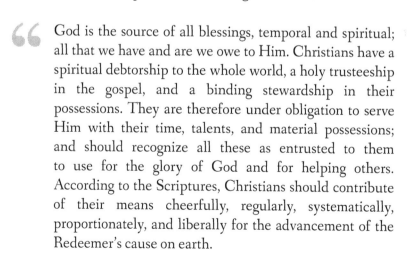 God is the source of all blessings, temporal and spiritual; all that we have and are we owe to Him. Christians have a spiritual debtorship to the whole world, a holy trusteeship in the gospel, and a binding stewardship in their possessions. They are therefore under obligation to serve Him with their time, talents, and material possessions; and should recognize all these as entrusted to them to use for the glory of God and for helping others. According to the Scriptures, Christians should contribute of their means cheerfully, regularly, systematically, proportionately, and liberally for the advancement of the Redeemer's cause on earth.

Comparing 1925/1963/2000

⇒ Article XXIV of the BF&M 1925 is titled "Stewardship." It corresponds with Article XIII in the 1963 and 2000 editions and reads similarly.

⇒ The 1963 and 2000 editions of this article read identically.[1]

⇒ See Appendix 1 for a side-by-side comparison.

Faithful Management

Stewardship is not ownership. Good stewards faithfully manage what belongs to someone else and readily understand they are accountable to the owner.

The Bible makes this clear. A steward is responsible for something that belongs to another (Gen. 43:19; 44:4; Matt. 20:8). Often, stewards are servants placed over other servants, as well as over their owners' property (Luke 16:1).

Regarding spiritual matters, the apostle Paul refers to himself, Apollos, and Peter as "servants of Christ and managers of the mysteries of God" (1 Cor. 4:1-2). Pastors are overseers of "God's household" (Tit. 1:7). And in a broader sense, all Christians are to be "good stewards of the varied grace of God" (1 Pet. 4:10).

The very idea of stewardship may be traced to the garden of Eden, where God commands Adam and Eve, "Be fruitful, multiply, fill the earth, and subdue it" (Gen. 1:28). Although the first humans rebel and plunge creation beneath the curse of sin, God continues to entrust mankind with stewardship of the earth. All of this is grounded in the truth that God owns everything and that human beings will give an account for our use and protection of all he has delegated to us.

Christians bear an even greater privilege in stewardship, for we are citizens of God's kingdom and trustees of the gospel. We are "bought at a price." Therefore, we belong to Christ, and everything we have – including our bodies – is at his disposal (1 Cor. 6:19-20).

Jesus stresses the importance of faithful stewardship in his parables.

The parable of the talents illustrates that true disciples are rewarded for their service, while false professors of the faith expose their unbelief through infidelity (Matt. 25:14-30).

The parable of the rich fool reveals the consequences of storing up treasures for oneself, with little or no regard for the one who owns the cattle on a thousand hills (Luke 12:16-21; cf. Ps. 50:10).

And the parable of the dishonest manager (Luke 16:1-13) demonstrates that "an abuse of stewardship indicates that one is not a Christian ... a matter for sober contemplation," according to Herschel Hobbs.[2]

There is a sense in which all Christians, like Paul, are obligated to the entire world (see Rom. 1:14). That is, we are commanded to yield ourselves and our material possessions so that others may come to know Christ. We are not to love the world – the global system over which Satan rules – or the things relating to it, for these are temporary and passing away (1 John 2:15-17). Christ came to set us free from the tyranny of things.

Stewardship and the Church

God commanded his people under the Old Covenant to tithe, or to give one-tenth of their increase to him. The Mosaic Law required Israelites to give tithes totaling more than 22 percent of their income each year, usually in the form of crops or animals.

There was the *Levitical tithe* to support those who offered daily sacrifices on behalf of the people (Lev. 27:30-33; Num. 18:21). Next, there was the *festival tithe* in which Israelites brought food for themselves and the Levites on special feast days (Deut. 14:22-27). Finally, there was the *welfare tithe*, offered every third year for the Levite, foreigner, orphan, and widow (Deut. 14:28-29). In addition, there were *freewill offerings* (Exod. 25:2; 1 Chron. 29:9).

There is some question as to whether these requirements under the Mosaic Law carry forward to the church today. And while we may vigorously debate this, a careful study of the New Testament shows that first-century believers probably gave more than ten percent – not because they were commanded to do so, but because they wanted to do so.

Consider how the New Testament says we should give:

Locally. Paul instructs believers at Corinth the same way he instructed the churches of Galatia – to set in store a collection for safe keeping (1 Cor. 16:1-2).

Consistently. Corinthian believers are urged to take up a weekly collection for their brothers and sisters in Jerusalem (1 Cor. 16:2-3).

Proportionately. We should give as God has prospered us (1 Cor. 16:2).

Sacrificially. Jesus praises the poor widow who gave two small coins (Luke 21:1-4). Paul commends the Macedonians for giving to the saints in Jerusalem out of their deep poverty (2 Cor. 8:2).

Liberally. We reap in proportion to what we sow (Luke 6:38; 2 Cor. 9:6).

Cheerfully. God loves those who give cheerfully – literally, in a hilarious spirit (2 Cor. 9:7).

The principles of stewardship Jesus and the apostles set forth show that when we give in the ways listed above, we fulfill Scripture's highest commands: to love God and love others.

As Hobbs notes, "The Lord measures the gift by the love and sacrifice it involves. He does not look simply at what one has before he gives but at what he has left after he has given."[3]

Questions for Personal or Group Study

1. What's the difference between *ownership* and *management*?

2. Where did the idea of stewardship begin?

3. Match the following parables of Jesus to the stewardship application:

Parable of the talents (Matt. 25:14-30)	There are dire consequences for storing up treasures for oneself.
Parable of the rich fool (Luke 12:16-21)	An abuse of stewardship reveals that one is not truly a Christian.
Parable of the dishonest manager (Luke 16:1-13)	True disciples are rewarded for their faithfulness; false professors of the faith expose their unbelief through infidelity.

4. What were the required Old Testament tithes, totaling more than 22 percent of an Israelite's income? Do you believe these tithes are required of Christians today?

5. Write in the principles of giving that match the New Testament passages below:

	Christians should give ...
Luke 6:38; 2 Corinthians 9:6	
Luke 21:1-4; 2 Corinthians 8:2	
1 Corinthians 16:1	
1 Corinthians 16:2	
2 Corinthians 9:7	

Devotional Prayer

Eternal Father,
owner of the cattle on a thousand hills,
generous to all who labor in your vineyards,
and just in demanding faithful stewardship ...
We manage what belongs to you –
our time, talents, and spiritual gifts;
our families, friendships, and commerce;
our income, investments, and properties.
As the apostles were servants of Christ
and managers of the mysteries of God,
and as pastors are overseers of God's household,
may all followers of Jesus be good stewards
of the varied grace of God.
We are bought at a price;
therefore, we belong to Christ,
and everything we have is at his disposal.
May we not fill our barns or swell our coffers
at the expense of storing up treasure in heaven.
May we understand that you don't regard
what we have before we give
but what remains afterward.

> — *Ps. 50:10; Matt. 6:19-20; 20:1-16; 1 Cor. 4:1-2;*
> *6:19-20; Tit. 1:7; 1 Pet. 4:10*

For Southern Baptists, cooperation plays
out on three levels: the association, the
state convention, and the Southern Baptist
Convention. A local church may affiliate
with any of these three networks.

Article XIV
Cooperation

Southern Baptists realize the limitations of their own local-church resources and understand that joining hands with other like-minded churches enables them to accomplish more together than they ever could alone.

Article XIV of *The Baptist Faith & Message 2000* reads:

 Christ's people should, as occasion requires, organize such associations and conventions as may best secure cooperation for the great objects of the Kingdom of God. Such organizations have no authority over one another or over the churches. They are voluntary and advisory bodies designed to elicit, combine, and direct the energies of our people in the most effective manner. Members of New Testament churches should cooperate with one another in carrying forward the missionary, educational, and benevolent ministries for the extension of Christ's Kingdom. Christian unity in the New Testament sense is spiritual harmony and voluntary cooperation for common ends by various groups of Christ's people. Cooperation is desirable between the various Christian denominations, when the end to be attained is itself justified, and when such cooperation involves no violation of conscience or compromise of loyalty to Christ and His Word as revealed in the New Testament.

Comparing 1925/1963/2000

⇒ Article XXII of the BF&M 1925 is titled "Co-Operation." It corresponds with Article XIV in the 1963 and 2000 editions.

⇒ The 1963 and 2000 editions of this article read nearly identically, and both are very similar to the 1925 version.[1]

⇒ See Appendix 1 for a side-by-side comparison.

Independent but Cooperating

Southern Baptists cling tenaciously to the doctrines of soul competency and the autonomy of the local church. At the same time, they embrace the Baptist distinctive of voluntary cooperation. As Herschel Hobbs puts it, "Baptists are an independent but cooperating people."[2]

Members of local Southern Baptist churches work together for the sake of the gospel in their communities. They also realize the limitations of their own resources and understand that joining hands with other like-minded churches enables them to accomplish more together than they ever could alone.

This idea of voluntary cooperation is rooted both in Scripture and Baptist tradition. Perhaps the earliest New Testament example is the Jerusalem Council in AD 49, which was convened to address doctrinal purity (Acts 15; Gal. 2). Representatives of the churches in Antioch and Jerusalem met voluntarily to discuss the Judaizer controversy. They respected each other's autonomy while reaching an agreement that preserved both unity in fellowship and the doctrinal conviction of salvation by grace alone, through faith alone, in Christ alone.

Another example is the apostle Paul's plea to the churches of Macedonia and Greece to gather funds for the relief of suffering Jewish

Christians in Jerusalem (1 Cor. 16:1; 2 Cor. 8-9). This was a voluntary offering. And though the Macedonians themselves faced economic distress, they "begged us earnestly for the privilege of sharing in the ministry to the saints" (2 Cor. 8:4).

A Biblical Model

Baptist churches traditionally have followed this biblical model. For example, the first Baptist churches in London organized themselves into an association. This enabled them to enjoy wider fellowship and share a mutual commitment to the gospel message.

In the United States, the first organized convention of Baptists arose from a desire to take the gospel to other nations. In 1812 in Philadelphia, Baptists organized the Baptist Society for the Propagation of the Gospel in Foreign Parts, which resulted in the founding of the Baptist General Convention.

The issue of slavery and a concern that the convention was becoming a centralized governing authority ultimately led to the convention's dissolution. But cooperative work continued through various mission societies and new conventions, including the Southern Baptist Convention (SBC).

The SBC was birthed in 1845 from a pro-slavery mindset – specifically, the view that slaveholders could serve as missionaries – and this left a perpetual stain on Southern Baptists' reputation, despite remarkable advances in global evangelism and missions. Messengers to the 1995 annual meeting of Southern Baptists formally acknowledged and repented of their historic support of slavery and racial segregation.

Three Levels of Cooperation

For Southern Baptists, cooperation plays out on three levels: the association, the state convention, and the Southern Baptist Convention. A local church may affiliate with any of these three networks. Typically, it does so with all three, but it is not required to do so.

Associations are networks of churches in a geographical region such as a county or a group of neighboring counties. Currently, there are more than 1,100 associations in the SBC.

State conventions are networks of churches across a state or, in some cases, a region such as the northwest United States. Nearly 1,800 churches are affiliated with the Missouri Baptist Convention. There are forty-one SBC-affiliated state conventions.

The Southern Baptist Convention is a network of roughly 47,000 self-governing churches that work together "for the purpose of proclaiming the Gospel of Jesus Christ to all people everywhere."[3]

Each level of cooperation embraces kingdom tasks for which it is uniquely suited. For example, the Southern Baptist Convention carries out evangelism, church-planting, and human-needs ministries on a global scale, coordinating the work of nine thousand full-time missionaries through the North American Mission Board and the International Mission Board. The SBC also operates six theological seminaries, promotes ethics and religious liberty on a national scale, and runs the day-to-day business of the convention through an elected Executive Committee.

The SBC may affiliate with other Christian denominations "when the end to be attained is itself justified, and when such cooperation involves no violation of conscience or compromise of loyalty to Christ and His Word as revealed in the New Testament," according to Article XIV of *The Baptist Faith & Message 2000.*

By the same token, Southern Baptists generally don't partner with groups or ministries that embrace a different doctrine of salvation or do not accept the Bible as the word of God.

But how do Southern Baptists pay for this cooperative kingdom work that extends from the local church to the ends of the earth? Through an amazing, collaborative innovation called the Cooperative Program (CP). The Cooperative Program is the funding process Southern Baptists have used since 1925 to support missions at the state, national, and international levels. Through CP, the ministry reach of each local church extends around the world as 47,000 cooperating Southern Baptist churches join hands to fulfill the Great Commission.

To learn more about CP, visit mobaptist.org/cp, or see Appendix II, "Missouri Baptists and the Cooperative Program."

Questions for Personal or Group Study

1. If Southern Baptist churches are autonomous, why do their members place such a high value on voluntary cooperation?

2. Share two first-century examples of voluntary cooperation among Christian churches. Consider Acts 15 and Galatians 2, along with 1 Corinthians 16:1 and 2 Corinthians 8-9.

3. Mark the following statements true or false:

_____ Southern Baptists follow a New Testament model of voluntary cooperation.

_____ In the United States, the first organized convention of Baptists arose from a desire to take the gospel to other nations.

_____ The Southern Baptist Convention was birthed in 1845 as an abolitionist movement.

_____ Southern Baptists send out roughly nine thousand full-time missionaries through the combined efforts of the North American Mission Board and the International Mission Board.

_____ To be a Southern Baptist church, a local congregation is required to affiliate with an association, a state convention, and the Southern Baptist Convention.

_____ The Southern Baptist Convention is a network of 47,000 cooperating churches.

4. Match the following Southern Baptist networks with their corresponding descriptions:

Associations	Networks of Baptist churches across a state or, in some cases, a region such as the northwest United States
State conventions	Networks of churches in a geographical region such as a county or a group of neighboring counties
Southern Baptist Convention	A network of roughly 47,000 independent churches that work together for the purpose of proclaiming the gospel of Jesus Christ to all people everywhere

5. What is the Cooperative Program? What makes it unique?

Devotional Prayer

O sovereign Trinity:
Father of all humanity,
Son of God and Son of Man,
Interceding Spirit,
three eternal, divine persons who collaborate
in creation, redemption, revelation, and restoration ...
May we always stand in awe
of your distinction in persons
yet unity in nature and purpose.
May we see that you created us for relationships –
with you and with one another.
May we look to the selfless labor
of the persons within the Godhead
and model our lives after them.
May we understand that a cord of three strands
is not easily broken;
that without you we can do nothing;
and that working together as adopted children of the Father
and Spirit-indwelt followers of Jesus,
we can accomplish more for your kingdom
than we ever could in our own strength.

— Eccles. 4:12; Dan. 7:9, 13-14; John 15:5; 17:5; Acts
17:28-29; Rom. 8:26-27

Jesus prayed, not that the Father would remove us from this world, but that he would protect us from the evil one, sanctify us in truth, and send us into the world to be salt and light.

Article XV
The Christian and the Social Order

The Bible instructs Christians to value our neighbors, society, and nation. This means taking an active role in the laws, customs, and moral fabric of our society.

Article XV of *The Baptist Faith & Message 2000* reads:

 All Christians are under obligation to seek to make the will of Christ supreme in our own lives and in human society. Means and methods used for the improvement of society and the establishment of righteousness among men can be truly and permanently helpful only when they are rooted in the regeneration of the individual by the saving grace of God in Jesus Christ. In the spirit of Christ, Christians should oppose racism, every form of greed, selfishness, and vice, and all forms of sexual immorality, including adultery, homosexuality, and pornography. We should work to provide for the orphaned, the needy, the abused, the aged, the helpless, and the sick. We should speak on behalf of the unborn and contend for the sanctity of all human life from conception to natural death. Every Christian should seek to bring industry, government, and society as a whole under the sway of the principles of righteousness, truth, and brotherly love. In order to promote these ends Christians should be ready to work with all men of good will in any good cause, always being careful to act in the spirit of love without compromising their loyalty to Christ and His truth.

Comparing 1925/1963/2000

⇒ Article XXI of the BF&M 1925 is titled "Social Service." It corresponds with Article XV in the 1963 and 2000 editions.

⇒ The 2000 edition of this article is more lengthy than its predecessors, in part because it reflects greater sensitivity to emerging cultural issues. For example, a portion of the 1963 version says Christians should oppose "every form of greed, selfishness, and vice." By comparison, the 2000 edition says Christians should oppose "racism, every form of greed, selfishness, and vice, and all forms of sexual immorality, including adultery, homosexuality, and pornography."

⇒ Further, the BF&M 2000, drafted nearly three decades after the landmark Roe v. Wade Supreme Court decision in 1973, and reflecting new trends in euthanasia, adds: "We should speak on behalf of the unborn and contend for the sanctity of all human life from conception to natural death."[1]

⇒ See Appendix 1 for a side-by-side comparison.

Being Salt and Light

Human beings cannot be made right with God through political processes, social programs, or religious affiliations. Only the transforming grace of Jesus Christ, the power of the gospel message, and the regenerating work of the Holy Spirit are able to breathe new life into the spiritually dead and make them adopted children of God the Father.

Even so, the Bible instructs Christians to value our neighbors, society, and nation. As the apostle Paul writes, "If possible, as far as it depends on you, live at peace with everyone" (Rom. 12:18). This means taking an active role in the laws, customs, and moral fabric of our society.

As followers of Jesus, we begin by confessing that we are redeemed sinners who have not yet been fully conformed to the image of Christ. Put more plainly, we are far from perfect. Further, we live in a sinful and fallen world that groans beneath the weight of sin and waits eagerly for the return of Jesus to set things right (see Rom. 8:18-23).

Jesus prayed, not that the Father would remove us from this world, but that he would protect us from the evil one, sanctify us in truth, and send us into the world to be salt and light (John 17:15-19; cf. Matt. 5:13-16). While we lack the power to create new heavens and a new earth, where righteousness dwells (2 Pet. 3:13), we are given the privilege of bearing testimony of the one who, one day, makes all things new (Rev. 21:5).

A God-ordained Purpose

The Bible teaches that government has a legitimate, God-ordained purpose in promoting good and punishing evil (Rom. 13:1-7). Even the first-century Roman Empire, with its cult of Caesar worship, infanticide, and oppression, operated under the sovereign hand of God to maintain order, build roads, and advance commerce – all of which enabled followers of Jesus to spread the gospel.

Perhaps, this prompted Peter to write:

 Submit to every human authority because of the Lord, whether to the emperor as the supreme authority or to governors as those sent out by him to punish those who do what is evil and to praise those who do what is good. For it is God's will that you silence the ignorance of foolish people by doing good. Submit as free people, not using your freedom as a cover-up for evil, but as God's slaves.

Honor everyone. Love the brothers and sisters. Fear God. Honor the emperor (1 Pet. 2:13-17).

Christians today bear the responsibility to engage the political and social order in ways that are faithful to Christ and his commands, knowing that these systems are tarnished and temporary. As Charles Kelley, Richard Land, and Albert Mohler write, "We understand that the church is the eternal people of God and the only institution on earth that will exist in the age to come. Governments and social orders will pass away, just as history records the rising and falling of countless empires, kingdoms, and nations."[2]

Herschel Hobbs points out that Jesus sought to change society in a responsible, constructive way – not in anarchy. He began with the individual and worked his way into society. "Rather than picket the home of Zacchaeus, he entered it and led him to become his disciple. Thus he changed a crooked chief publican into a philanthropic tax commissioner (Luke 19:1-10)."[3]

Our Social Responsibility

The Baptist Faith & Message 2000 lists several areas of social responsibility the New Testament embraces, reminding us that we are to oppose:

Racism. This has been a blight in our nation's history, and in the chronicles of the Southern Baptist Convention. Racism denies the *Imago Dei* – the image of God – in which every person is created. And it runs counter to God's design for people of every kindred, tongue, and nation to worship before his throne in heaven (Rev. 5:9).

Greed. Christian stewardship requires us to regard everything God has entrusted to us – material wealth, time, talents, family, etc. – as belonging to God.

Selfishness. Contrary to the desires of our flesh, Christians should follow the example of Christ, who "did not come to be served, but to serve, and to give his life as a ransom for many" (Matt. 20:28).

Vice. Christians should speak against degrading practices as we model Christlikeness, being salt and light in a world that loves darkness.

Sexual immorality. In whatever form it takes – adultery, homosexuality, pornography, etc. – sexual immorality "robs God of the glory that is rightfully His through the proper exercise of the sexual gift" (Exod. 20:14; Heb. 13:4).[4]

At the same time, Christians should work to improve the lives of the most vulnerable among us: the orphaned, needy, abused, aged, helpless, and sick. Southern Baptists in general, and Missouri Baptists in particular, address these needs through foster care and adoption ministries; rescue from human trafficking; homes for the aged; hospice care; healthcare ministries; disaster relief; feeding programs; help for refugees, and much more. These ministries are funded in part through the Cooperative Program and the Missouri Missions Offering, and they're sustained by professional and volunteer labor.

Southern Baptists often partner with non-SBC ministries, and even with secular organizations, to serve people in need. This is carried out in the spirit of Christlike love without compromising loyalty to Christ or biblical fidelity.

As M. E. Dodd, SBC president from 1934-35, once wrote:

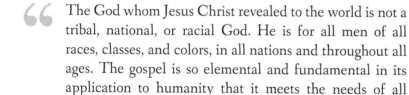 The God whom Jesus Christ revealed to the world is not a tribal, national, or racial God. He is for all men of all races, classes, and colors, in all nations and throughout all ages. The gospel is so elemental and fundamental in its application to humanity that it meets the needs of all kinds of persons in all places and at all times.[5]

Christians are citizens of the kingdom of God. We're also citizens of a nation, state, and community. We should seek to be good citizens of them all.

Questions for Personal or Group Study

1. Mark the following statements true or false:

_____ God uses political processes, social programs, and religious affiliations to make people right with him.

_____ Governments have a legitimate, God-ordained purpose in promoting good and punishing evil, even when these governments are corrupt.

_____ Jesus sought to change society in a responsible, constructive way.

_____ Southern Baptists should oppose racism, greed, selfishness, vice, and all forms of sexual immorality.

_____ While we should seek to live in peace with all people, Southern Baptists must never partner with non-Southern Baptists in social or political initiatives.

_____ Christians are citizens of the kingdom of God. Therefore, we should not involve ourselves in political activities of any kind.

2. Read Romans 8:18-23 and 12:18. What do these two passages tell us about the world in which we live and our responsibility as Christians until Jesus returns?

3. Match the following Southern Baptist organizations with their corresponding ministries to help the most vulnerable among us:

Children's Homes	Senior adult care; hospice care
Baptist Homes	Foster care; adoption; orphan care; rescue from human trafficking; crisis pregnancy counseling
Hospitals / Clinics	Disaster relief; feeding programs; refugee assistance
Relief Networks	Healthcare; wellness

4. Read 2 Peter 3:10-13 and Revelation 21:1-8. How do these passages of Scripture give us a divine perspective of how we should live our lives today?

5. Can you think of an example in which Southern Baptists partner with non-Southern Baptists to help the most vulnerable among us?

Devotional Prayer

O God of decency and order,
who created a universe that, though fallen,
still operates with incalculable precision;
who reveals himself in creation
as the divine designer,
and in conscience
as the divine moral law giver;
who established authorities in the home,
community, and nation
to promote good and punish evil ...
May we strive to live in peace with everyone;
grasp the reality that our world groans
beneath the weight of sin
and waits eagerly for the return of Jesus
to set things right;
be salt and light in a sinful and fallen world;
engage the political and social order
in ways that are faithful to Christ
and to his commands;
oppose racism, greed,
selfishness, vice, and sexual immorality;
work to improve the lives
of the most vulnerable among us;
and bear testimony of the one who, one day,
makes all things new.

— Matt. 5:13-16; Rom. 8:18-23; 12:18; 13:1-7; 1 Cor.
14:40; Rev. 21:5

Article XVI
Peace and War

The reconciliation of people to God must precede reconciliation of people to one another. We cannot truly live at peace with our neighbors until "the God of peace" resides in our hearts.

— Romans 15:33

Article XVI of *The Baptist Faith & Message* 2000 reads:

 It is the duty of Christians to seek peace with all men on principles of righteousness. In accordance with the spirit and teachings of Christ they should do all in their power to put an end to war.

The true remedy for the war spirit is the gospel of our Lord. The supreme need of the world is the acceptance of His teachings in all the affairs of men and nations, and the practical application of His law of love. Christian people throughout the world should pray for the reign of the Prince of Peace.

Comparing 1925/1963/2000

⇒ Article XIX of the BF&M 1925 is titled "Peace and War." It corresponds with Article XVI in the 1963 and 2000 editions.

⇒ All three versions of this article are quite similar.

⇒ The 1963 and 2000 editions of this article read identically, except that the BF&M 2000 adds: "Christian people throughout the world should pray for the reign of the Prince of Peace."

⇒ The BF&M 1925 ends with these words: "We urge Christian people throughout the world to pray for the reign of the Prince of Peace, and to oppose everything likely to provoke war."[1]

⇒ See Appendix 1 for a side-by-side comparison.

Blessed are the Peacemakers

God's word commands Christians to love peace and to make peace. Jesus tells his listeners in the Sermon on the Mount, "Blessed are the peacemakers, for they will be called sons of God" (Matt. 5:9). And the apostle Paul instructs his Roman readers, "If possible, as far as it depends on you, live at peace with everyone" (Rom. 12:18).

Even so, followers of Jesus understand that conflicts of every kind have punctuated human history since the Fall. Adam and Eve's firstborn son, Cain, strikes his brother in a murderous rage, and the human race quickly descends into a spiral of personal, societal, and global conflict that continues today.

Over the last 3,400 years, humans have been entirely at peace for only 268 years, or just eight percent of recorded history, according to one source. At least 108 million people were killed in the wars of the twentieth century. And estimates of the total loss of life in wars throughout history range from 150 million to one billion.[2]

Add to this the war-induced spread of disease, displacement of people groups, reduced birthrates, and financial impact – World War II alone cost each American $20,388 – and it's clear that sinful and fallen people are our own worst enemies.[3]

The Prince of Peace himself said that "wars and rumors of wars" would characterize the present age (Matt. 24:6). Jesus offers no hope of lasting peace until he reigns supremely in our hearts and returns to earth one day to establish his kingdom in fullness. Even then, his glorious appearing is one of warfare against the wicked, who violently oppose his righteous rule (Rev. 19:11-21).

Reconciliation to God

So, how are Christians to regard war and peace as we wait eagerly for the Lord's return? We should begin by understanding that reconciliation of people to God must precede reconciliation of people to one another. We cannot truly live at peace with our neighbors until "the God of peace" resides in our hearts (Rom. 15:33).

Jesus was a peacemaker, not a pacifist.

Because Jesus bore our sins on the cross – including the sins that lead to warfare – we are declared in right standing with God by faith. Further, "we have peace with God through our Lord Jesus Christ" (Rom. 5:1). Jesus gave his life to establish the grounds for peace between God and people, and between people and people (2 Cor. 5:17-21; Eph. 2:13-17).

Jesus was a peacemaker, not a pacifist. He angrily confronted religious leaders who kept people bound in sin and human tradition. He pronounced woes on hypocritical scribes and Pharisees, including the judgment of hell (Matt. 23). He overturned the money-changers' tables at the temple and drove away those who sold sacrificial animals at inflated prices (Matt. 21:12-13; Mark 11:15-17; Luke 19:45-46; John 2:13-16). And when he returns to earth one day in the presence of holy angels and redeemed people, he wears a bloody robe and strikes the nations with the sword of his mouth (Rev. 19:13-15).

Just before his betrayal and arrest, Jesus instructs his followers to carry swords for self-defense, likely to ensure he is not taken before the appointed time (Luke 22:36-38). But a short time later, he rebukes Peter for taking the offense with a sword and cutting off the ear of the high priest's servant (Luke 22:49-51). Jesus' time had come to surrender to the necessity of the cross, and violence wielded in opposition to Christ's passion was rebellion against his Father's will.

So, it seems Jesus is not opposed to warfare when in self-defense – defense of home, family, the innocent. But warfare to advance sinful agendas is strictly prohibited in Scripture.

Just-war Theory

This often leads Christians to consider the concept of a "just war." Thomas Aquinas first developed the just-war theory in the thirteenth century, laying out the conditions for waging war and, if justified, how it should be waged.[4] Amended through the centuries, the just-war theory generally establishes the following criteria:

- There must be a just cause – that is, the use of force must be defensive in nature, not to acquire wealth or power.
- The intention must be to secure a fair, lasting peace for all parties.
- War must be waged as a last resort, when all other legitimate means of settling a conflict have been tried and have failed.
- The objectives must be limited to what is necessary to establish peace.

- A legitimate authority must approve and control the use of force.
- War should be waged with proportionality, with just enough force to achieve victory and only against legitimate targets; non-combatants are to be protected whenever possible.
- There must be a reasonable chance of success, along with a reasonable hope that the conflict leads to lasting peace.[5]

Warfare is a horrid scar on human history, and it will continue until Christ returns to put down all rebellion and establish his kingdom in righteousness and peace. Until then, we must seek to live at peace with others, engaging in warfare as a last resort in self-defense or the rescue of innocent parties.

At the same time, we should remember the words of Paul, exhorting us to understand that our enemy is neither human nor national, but spiritual: "For our struggle is not against flesh and blood, but against the rulers, against the authorities, against the cosmic powers of this darkness, against evil, spiritual forces in the heavens" (Eph. 6:12). For this cosmic battle, the Lord has granted us "the full armor of God" (see Eph. 6:11-18).

One day, all people will stand before Christ and give an account of our lives, including the degree to which we love and promote peace (see Ps. 4:8; Matt. 25:31-32; Rom. 14:10; 1 Cor. 4:5; 2 Cor. 5:10; 13:11; Col. 3:15; 1 Thess. 5:15; 2 Tim. 4:1; Heb. 9:27; 1 Pet. 3:11; Rev. 20:11-15; 22:12).

Questions for Personal or Group Study

1. When Jesus says, "Blessed are the peacemakers" (Matt. 5:9), is he prohibiting his followers from ever engaging in warfare? Why or why not?

2. Mark the following statements true or false:

_____ Human beings have been completely at peace with one another for only eight percent of recorded history.

_____ Martin Luther developed the just-war theory, which lays out conditions for when and how to wage war.

_____ Jesus was a pacifist.

_____ Jesus is not opposed to warfare when it's conducted in self-defense – for example, defense of home, family, and the innocent.

_____ Our real enemy is neither human nor national, but spiritual – specifically, Satan and evil spirits.

_____ Jesus offers no hope of lasting peace until he reigns supremely in our hearts and returns to earth one day to establish his kingdom in fullness.

3. Read Luke 22:36-38, 49-51. Is Jesus contradicting himself in these two passages of Scripture? How might you reconcile the command of Jesus to his disciples to carry swords with his rebuke of Peter for using a sword?

4. Which of the following are valid criteria for a just war:

(a) There must be a just cause – that is, the use of force must be defensive in nature, not to acquire wealth or power.

(b) The end justifies the means.

(c) War must be waged as a last resort.

(d) A legitimate authority must approve and control the use of force.

(e) War should be waged only when there is an overwhelming chance of victory.

(f) Non-combatants are fair game only if the other side started the conflict.

5. Match the following passages of Scripture to their corresponding truths:

Matthew 24:6	Jesus returns wearing a blood-stained robe, destroying his enemies with the sword from his mouth.
Romans 12:18	The Christian's battle is not against flesh and blood but against "evil, spiritual forces in the heavens."
Ephesians 6:12	Christians should strive to live at peace with everyone.
Revelation 19:11-21	Wars and rumors of wars will characterize the present age until Christ returns.

Devotional Prayer

O Prince of Peace,
we live in a world at war,
and in a day when wars and rumors of wars
characterize this present evil age.
Our ultimate enemy is not the angry atheist,
the counterfeit Christian,
or the many antichrists
who persecute your church;
rather, it is the evil one,
who wages war as ruler of a world system
in rebellion against you.
He is a defeated foe,
for you have crushed him beneath your heel;
still, he carries out a scorched-earth campaign
to keep the lost in bondage
and the saved at bay.
All human conflicts are the wreckage
of Adam's sin,
but you have come as the last Adam
to set things right.
Until you return in blood-stained robes,
wielding the sword of your mouth
to vanquish wicked men and angels,
may we be blessed as peacemakers
and thus called the children of God.
Show us how, as far as it depends on us,
to live at peace with everyone.
Help us know we cannot truly live at peace
with our neighbors
until the God of peace resides in our hearts.

— Gen. 3:15; Isa. 9:6; Matt. 5:9; 24:6; John 12:31;
Rom. 12:18; 15:33; 1 Cor. 15:45; 2 Tim. 2:26; Rev.
19:13-15

Religious liberty is neither a license
to live recklessly, with no regard for
others, nor mere toleration of those who
believe differently.

Article XVII
Religious Liberty

Practically speaking, religious liberty means equality before the law for Christians and non-Christians alike. It means the freedom to worship God, or not to worship God.

Article XVII of *The Baptist Faith & Message* 2000 reads:

 God alone is Lord of the conscience, and He has left it free from the doctrines and commandments of men which are contrary to His Word or not contained in it. Church and state should be separate. The state owes to every church protection and full freedom in the pursuit of its spiritual ends. In providing for such freedom no ecclesiastical group or denomination should be favored by the state more than others. Civil government being ordained of God, it is the duty of Christians to render loyal obedience thereto in all things not contrary to the revealed will of God. The church should not resort to the civil power to carry on its work. The gospel of Christ contemplates spiritual means alone for the pursuit of its ends. The state has no right to impose penalties for religious opinions of any kind. The state has no right to impose taxes for the support of any form of religion. A free church in a free state is the Christian ideal, and this implies the right of free and unhindered access to God on the part of all men, and the right to form and propagate opinions in the sphere of religion without interference by the civil power.

Comparing 1925/1963/2000

⇒ Article XVIII of the BF&M 1925 is titled "Religious Liberty." It corresponds with Article XVII in the 1963 and 2000 editions.

⇒ All three versions of this article are nearly identical.[1]

⇒ See Appendix 1 for a side-by-side comparison.

The Mother of All True Freedom

Religious liberty is the God-given right of all people to worship according to their consciences. As Herschel Hobbs writes:

Religious liberty is the mother of all true freedom. It is rooted in the very nature of both God and man created in God's likeness. It implies the competency of the soul in religion, and denies to any person, civil government, or religious system the right to come between God and man.[2]

Practically speaking, religious liberty means equality before the law for Christians and non-Christians alike. It means the freedom to worship God, or not to worship God. If our creator does not compel us to acknowledge him in this life, no human being should force another to adopt any belief system, no matter how true or widely held.

At the same time, the Bible is clear that our beliefs have consequences – in this life and in the life to come. One day, all people will stand before God and give an account of our lives – not just what we believed, but how we acted on those beliefs (see Dan. 12:2; Rom. 14:10; 1 Cor. 4:5; 2 Cor. 5:10; 2 Thess. 1:6-7; Heb. 9:27; Rev. 20:11-15; 22:12).

That means religious liberty is neither a license to live recklessly, with no regard for others, nor mere toleration of those who believe differently. Religious liberty does not stand on political platforms or hang from legal pillars. While civil authorities may proclaim religious tolerance, only God may grant religious freedom.

George W. Truett, longtime pastor of First Baptist Church in Dallas and president of the Southern Baptist Convention from 1927-1929, preached a message from the steps of the U.S. Capitol in 1920. In part, he proclaimed:

 Our contention is not for mere toleration, but for absolute liberty. There is a wide difference between toleration and liberty.... Toleration is a matter of expediency, while liberty is a matter of principle. Toleration is a gift from man, while liberty is a gift from God.... God wants free worshipers and no other kind.[3]

Liberty and Lordship

True liberty is grounded in the lordship of Christ. As Jesus tells the religious leaders who oppose him, "So if the Son sets you free, you really will be free" (John 8:36). Paul picks up on this in Romans 8:1-2: "Therefore, there is now no condemnation for those in Christ Jesus, because the law of the Spirit of life in Christ Jesus has set you free from the law of sin and death."

While Christ sets us free, we are to exercise our freedom under the sovereign guidance of the Holy Spirit and according to biblical principles (Rom. 8:5-9; 2 Cor. 3:17). Therefore, when human commandments run contrary to God's expressed will in Scripture, Christians should obey God (Acts 4:18-20).

The New Testament writers instruct us to respect those in authority over us. We are to pray for our leaders (1 Tim. 2:1-2), honor them (1 Pet. 2:13-17), and submit to their authority (Rom. 13:1-7).

However, when people in authority command Christians to do something God forbids, or forbid us from doing something God commands, we may rightly respond, as Peter tells the high priest who wants to silence him, "We must obey God rather than people" (Acts 5:29).

Separation of Church and State

Christ sets the boundaries between church and state. He makes this clear when the religious elite press him to decide between allegiance to Rome and the Jewish faith: "Give, then, to Caesar the things that are Caesar's, and to God the things that are God's" (Matt. 22:21).

This doesn't mean there are no grounds for relationships between religious organizations and civil authorities. Jesus acknowledged the rights and responsibilities of the state (Matt. 22:15-21). First-century Christians benefited from the Roman Empire's roads, aqueducts, and other infrastructure. At times, they appealed to Rome for protection (Acts 18:12-17; 21:27-39; 22:25-30; 25:10-12). And both Paul and Peter instructed their readers to submit to the state's authority (Rom. 13:1-8; 1 Pet. 2:13-17).

The church should produce the kinds of citizens that enhance a free society and improve an oppressive one.

Today, federal, state, and local authorities support an atmosphere in which the church can thrive, providing fire and police protection, national defense, and social stability. In turn, the church should produce the kinds of citizens that enhance a free society and improve an oppressive one.

At the same time, the church and the state operate in mutually exclusive realms. Neither should seek to control the other to accomplish its goals. Christ has not commanded the church to muster armies or supply power grids, but to take the gospel to the ends of the earth (Acts 1:8). And the state has no God-given right to leverage the church for political ends, or to favor one religion over another.

Separation of church and state does not mean religious beliefs and expressions are to be banned from the public square. Rather, it acknowledges the mutually beneficial coexistence of both church and state, and it recognizes the unique function of both.

Baptists have always championed religious liberty. The roots of modern Baptist churches are found in the Separatist movement in England and Holland. In the U.S., Roger Williams established the colony of Rhode Island with a charter calling for absolute religious liberty. And the insistence of Virginia Baptists that religious liberty be written into our nation's governing documents contributed to the First Amendment of the U.S. Constitution.[4]

Today, Southern Baptists support religious liberty in part through the Ethics & Religious Liberty Commission (ERLC), a Cooperative Program-funded ministry dedicated to engaging the culture with the gospel and speaking to issues in the public square for the protection of religious liberty and human flourishing. The ERLC has offices in Washington, D.C. and Nashville, Tenn. Learn more online at erlc.com.

Questions for Personal or Group Study

1. How would you describe religious liberty in a few short sentences?

2. Match the following passages of Scripture to their corresponding instructions to Christians regarding our obligation to civil authorities:

Matthew 22:21	We should honor those in authority over us – even corrupt rulers.
Acts 5:29	We should submit to those in authority over us.
Romans 13:1-7	We should pray for our leaders.
1 Timothy 2:1-2	We should pay our taxes.
1 Peter 2:13-17	When the commands of any authority conflict with the clear teachings of Scripture, we must obey God rather than people.

3. Mark the following statements about the separation of church and state true or false:

_____ There is no basis for relationships of any kind between religious organizations and civil authorities.

_____ The church and the state operate in mutually exclusive realms. Neither should seek to control the other to accomplish its goals.

_____ Christ sets the boundaries between church and state.

_____ Separation of church and state means religious beliefs and expressions are to be banned from the public square.

_____ First-century Christians benefited from the Roman Empire's roads, aqueducts, and other infrastructure. At times, they even appealed to Rome for protection.

_____ Christ has not commanded the church to muster armies or supply power grids, but to take the gospel to the ends of the earth.

4. What would you say is a good rule of thumb for determining when it's okay to disobey those in authority over us?

5. Read Romans 13:1-8 and 1 Peter 2:13-17. What do Paul and Peter say about the benefits of civil authorities?

Devotional Prayer

O Lord of Liberty,
the one who sets us free
from the law of sin and death ...
May we exercise our freedom
under the sovereign guidance of your Spirit
and according to the principles of your word.
May we respect those in authority over us,
while maintaining a willingness
to obey God rather than people
when they command us to do something you forbid
or forbid us to do something you command.
May we recognize the boundaries
Christ established between church and state,
while acknowledging the unique functions of both.
May we champion religious liberty
for the Christ-follower and Christ-denier alike,
while seeking to ensure that no human authority
impedes the taking of the gospel
to the ends of the earth.

— Matt. 22:21; John 8:36; Acts 1:8; 5:29; Rom. 8:1-2,
5-9; 2 Cor. 3:17

Article XVIII
The Family

Marriage, family, and gender are gifts from God. They are established for the good of all people, who are created in the image of God.

Article XVIII of *The Baptist Faith & Message* 2000 reads:

 God has ordained the family as the foundational institution of human society. It is composed of persons related to one another by marriage, blood, or adoption.

Marriage is the uniting of one man and one woman in covenant commitment for a lifetime. It is God's unique gift to reveal the union between Christ and His church and to provide for the man and the woman in marriage the framework for intimate companionship, the channel of sexual expression according to biblical standards, and the means for procreation of the human race.

The husband and wife are of equal worth before God, since both are created in God's image. The marriage relationship models the way God relates to His people. A husband is to love his wife as Christ loved the church. He has the God-given responsibility to provide for, to protect, and to lead his family. A wife is to submit herself graciously to the servant leadership of her husband even as the church willingly submits to the headship of Christ. She, being in the image of God as is her husband and thus equal to him, has the God-given responsibility to respect her husband and to serve as his helper in managing the household and nurturing the next generation.

Children, from the moment of conception, are a blessing and heritage from the Lord. Parents are to demonstrate to their children God's pattern for marriage. Parents are to teach their children spiritual and moral values and to lead them, through consistent lifestyle example and loving discipline, to make choices based on biblical truth. Children are to honor and obey their parents.

Comparing 1925/1963/2000

⇒ The BF&M 1925 did not specifically address the topic of the family.

⇒ This article was added to the BF&M 1963 through an amendment in 1998.

⇒ The amended 1963 and 2000 editions of Article XVIII read almost identically, with one notable exception: In paragraph two, the most recent version adds that marriage is "God's unique gift to reveal the union between Christ and His church ...."[1]

⇒ See Appendix 1 for a side-by-side comparison.

God's Unchanging Standards

Southern Baptists added Article XVIII to the *Baptist Faith & Message* in 1998, thus making it part of the 1963 confession and carrying it forward into the 2000 edition. Witnessing the erosion of our culture's view of marriage, family, and gender, Southern Baptists boldly reaffirmed God's unchanging standards as revealed in Scripture and embraced by Christians throughout the centuries.

Today, the prevailing secular view is that marriage is an archaic, man-made institution in need of revision – or even demolition. Modern society also sees the family as an evolutionary unit that may be restructured to meet changing societal needs, and gender as a fluid, personal choice.

But the Bible says otherwise. Marriage, family, and gender are gifts from God. They are established for the good of all people, who are created in the image of God (Gen. 1:27).

Marriage

Marriage is the first institution God ordains, and he does so before the Fall (see Gen. 2:18-25). The consistent standard of Scripture is that marriage is the uniting of one man and one woman in covenant commitment for a lifetime. The gift of sexual intimacy is for pleasure and procreation within the confines of monogamous marriage, requiring unselfishness and purity (see Heb. 13:4).

When biblical figures – even heroes like King David – engage in sexual activity outside the bonds of marriage, it ends badly. Polygamy proves no less a sin. As Charles Kelley, Richard Land, and Albert Mohler write, "The shared gift of intimacy, which is a blessing to a husband and wife within the marital covenant, can only lead to destruction and heartbreak outside marriage (see 1 Cor. 7:1-16)."[2]

Further, marriage should be highly prized, for it is given to us as a metaphor for the relationship between Christ and his church. The Lord Jesus is depicted as the bridegroom, and his church is the bride (see Matt. 9:15; John 3:29; 2 Cor. 11:3; Rev. 19:7; 21:2; 22:17; cf. Matt. 25:1-13).

The apostle Paul develops this concept more fully in his letter to the Ephesians, where he instructs wives to submit to their husbands "as to the Lord, because the husband is the head of the wife as Christ is the head of the church." He goes on to say, "Husbands, love your wives, just as Christ loved the church and gave himself for her" (Eph. 5:22-23, 25).

Paul links marriage and the church back to the garden of Eden and God's creative intent for fidelity in covenant relationships: "For this reason a man will leave his father and mother and be joined to his wife, and the two will become one flesh. This mystery is profound, but I am talking about Christ and the church" (Eph. 5:31-32).

Husbands are to provide for their families and protect them from harm. They also are to be the spiritual leaders in the marriage and family – not in a tyrannical sense, but on the basis of spiritual authority as demonstrated in the faithfulness of Jesus (see Col. 3:18-21).

Wives are equal partners in marriage, as both are created in the image of God. At the same time, a wife is to receive "the God-given responsibility to respect her husband and to serve as his helper in managing the household and nurturing the next generation."[3]

Family

Biblically, a family consists of persons related by marriage, blood, or adoption. A family, consisting of a father, a mother, and their children, "reflects God's glory in the right ordering of civilization and society."[4]

This means that family, like marriage, is central to God's design for humanity. It requires love, order, intimacy, and unity – qualities that have existed throughout eternity within the members of the Trinity.

"The family is not a laboratory for social experimentation but an arena in which God's glory is shown to the world in the right ordering of human relationships."

– *Kelley, Land, and Mohler*

All people, whether married or unmarried, are related to family through various ties of blood, kinship, or adoption. Yahweh is a relational God, and he made us to thrive in relationships as well.

He even adopts followers of Jesus as his sons and daughters (Rom. 8:14-17; Gal. 3:26; 4:6; Eph. 1:5). This is good for us to remember. In the ancient Near East, a person's family of origin and ancestry formed his or her primary identity. This continued for first-century Christians with an important twist: their identity was now the family of God gathered around Christ.

As Jonathan Pennington notes, "The most frequent metaphor used to describe Christians is 'brother and sister.' This family language is very purposeful, teaching Christians to realign their allegiances around their new identity as the children of God."[5]

Modern culture seeks to redefine the family and celebrate alternative expressions of it. Examples include same-sex marriage, cohabitation, polygamy, polyandry, and more. But as Kelley, Land, and Mohler explain, "The family is not a laboratory for social experimentation but an arena in which God's glory is shown to the world in the right ordering of human relationships."[6]

Children are to be welcomed as blessings from God. Parents have a God-ordained responsibility to raise them in the "training and instruction of the Lord" (Eph. 6:4). In return, children are to honor and obey their parents, which is pleasing to God (Exod. 20:12; Eph. 6:1-3).

Gender

Scripture is clear that God created human beings male and female, and he did so that we might be his image bearers (Gen. 1:26-27). This doesn't mean God, who is spirit, has gender, although the eternal Son of God became flesh as a man (John 1:14; 1 Tim. 2:5), and the other members of the Trinity are depicted in masculine terms in Scripture.

It does mean, however, that God created men and women in a complementary way for marriage and procreation. Further, their intimacy as husband and wife reflects the intimacy of the members of the Trinity, as well as the close bond between Christ and his church.

God defines gender. Humans redefine it at their peril. Gender may be confirmed through God-given physical evidence – genetic, biological, and anatomical, for example. Humans are to celebrate gender as a gift from God.

At the same time, gender confusion – including a condition known as *gender dysphoria* – is nearly as old as the Fall. Because human beings created in the image of God live in a fallen world, the lines between male and female are sometimes blurred – for example, in those rare instances when a person is born with both male and female features, and, more commonly, in those who feel intense emotional unease with their birth gender.

In every case, followers of Jesus are to treat those who struggle with gender confusion with compassion and understanding, knowing that we, too, are subject to frailties of our own. At the same time, we should help our friends rediscover God's gift of gender, sharing a biblical view of what it means to be men and women created in the image of God.

Questions for Personal or Group Study

1. What is a biblically faithful definition of marriage? How does sexual intimacy fit into marriage, according to Scripture?

2. In what ways is marriage a metaphor for the relationship between Christ and his church?

3. Mark the following statements about the family as true or false:

_____ Biblically, a family consists of persons related by marriage, blood, or adoption.

_____ Yahweh is a relational God, and he made us to thrive in relationships as well. He even adopts followers of Jesus as his sons and daughters.

_____ Cohabitation was frowned on in ancient Israel, but the apostles accepted it so as not to create problems in the church.

_____ Two people of the same gender married to one another can biblically form a family as long as they are committed to one another.

_____ Like marriage, family is central to God's design for humanity.

_____ Parents have a God-ordained responsibility to raise children to be just like they are.

4. Match the following passages of Scripture to their corresponding truth about marriage, family, and gender:

Genesis 1:26-27	Marriage is the first institution God ordains, and he does so before the Fall.
Genesis 2:18-25	Yahweh is a relational God, and he made us to thrive in relationships as well; he even adopts followers of Jesus as his sons and daughters.
Romans 8:14-17	Marriage should be highly prized, for it is given to us as a metaphor for the relationship between Christ and his church; the Lord Jesus is depicted as the bridegroom, and his church is the bride.
Hebrews 13:4	God created men and women in his image; that means the gifts of marriage, family, and gender are established and fixed for our good.
Revelation 19:7	The gift of sexual intimacy is for pleasure and procreation within the confines of monogamous marriage, requiring unselfishness and purity.

5. What is *gender confusion*? How should Christians treat those struggling with this condition?

Notes:

Devotional Prayer

Dearest Abba,
our Heavenly Father, who delights in his children
and bestows marriage, family, and gender
as gifts for the good of all people ...
We thank you for the institution of marriage,
uniting one man and one woman in covenant,
picturing the unbreakable relationship
between Christ and his Bride.
We thank you for the institution of family,
consisting of father, mother, and children,
reflecting your glory in the right ordering of society,
and depicting our adoption as your sons and daughters.
We thank you for creating us male and female
so that, as your complementary imagers,
we might marry and have children,
and in so doing display the unfading love
that exists between the persons of the Godhead.
May we value the intimacy of marriage,
the unity of family,
and the distinctions of gender
as the tender and timely gifts
that endure the assaults
of a dark and broken world.

— Gen. 2:18-25; Matt. 25:1-13; Rom. 8:14-17; Gal.
3:26; 4:6; Eph. 1:5; 5:22-23, 25, 31-32

Appendix I

Comparison Charts

The charts that begin on this page compare the 1925, 1963, and 2000 versions of *The Baptist Faith & Message*. Some articles feature explanatory notes at the bottom of a column. This information is obtained from the Southern Baptist Convention's official website and may be accessed at bfm.sbc.net/comparison-chart.

Preamble

1925	1963	2000
The report of the Committee on Statement of Baptist Faith and Message was presented as follows by E. Y. Mullins, Kentucky:	*Committee on Baptist Faith and Message*	The 1999 session of the Southern Baptist Convention, meeting in Atlanta, Georgia, adopted the following motion addressed to the President of the Convention:
Your committee begs leave to report as follows:	The 1962 session of the Southern Baptist Convention, meeting in San Francisco, California, adopted the following motion:	
Your committee recognizes that they were appointed "to consider	"Since the report of the Committee on Statement of Baptist Faith and	"I move that in your capacity as Southern Baptist Convention chairman, you appoint a

1925	1963	2000

the advisability of issuing another statement of the Baptist Faith and Message, and report at the next Convention."

In pursuance of the instructions of the Convention, and in consideration of the general denominational situation, your committee have decided to recommend the New Hampshire Confession of Faith, revised at certain points, and with some additional articles growing out of present needs, for approval by the Convention, in the event a statement of the Baptist faith and message is deemed necessary at this time.

The present occasion for a reaffirmation of Christian fundamentals is the prevalence of naturalism in the modern teaching and preaching of religion. Christianity is supernatural in its origin and history. We repudiate every theory of religion, which denies the supernatural elements in our faith.

As introductory to the doctrinal articles, we recommend the adoption by the Convention of the following statement of

Message was adopted in 1925, there have been various statements from time to time which have been made, but no over-all statement which might be helpful at this time as suggested in Section 2 of that report, or introductory statement which might be used as an interpretation of the 1925 Statement."

"We recommend, therefore, that the president of this Convention be requested to call a meeting of the men now serving as presidents of the various state conventions that would qualify as a member of the Southern Baptist Convention committee under Bylaw 18 to present to the Convention in Kansas City some similar statement which shall serve as information to the churches, and which may serve as guidelines to the various agencies of the Southern Baptist Convention. It is understood that any group or individuals may approach this committee to be of service. The expenses of this committee shall be borne by the Convention Operating Budget."

Your committee thus

blue ribbon committee to review the *Baptist Faith and Message* statement with the responsibility to report and bring any recommendations to this meeting next June in Orlando."

President Paige Patterson appointed the committee as follows: Max Barnett (OK), Steve Gaines (AL), Susie Hawkins (TX), Rudy A. Hernandez (TX), Charles S. Kelley, Jr. (LA), Heather King (IN), Richard D. Land (TN), Fred Luter (LA), R. Albert Mohler, Jr. (KY), T. C. Pinckney (VA), Nelson Price (GA), Adrian Rogers (TN), Roger Spradlin (CA), Simon Tsoi (AZ), Jerry Vines (FL). Adrian Rogers (TN) was appointed chairman.

Your committee thus constituted begs leave to present its report as follows:

Baptists are a people of deep beliefs and cherished doctrines. Throughout our history we have been a confessional people, adopting statements of faith as a witness to our beliefs and a pledge of our faithfulness to the doctrines revealed in Holy Scripture.

1925	1963	2000

1925

the historic Baptist conception of the nature and function of confessions of faith in our religious and denominational life, believing that some such statement will clarify the atmosphere and remove some causes of misunderstanding, friction, and apprehension. Baptists approve and circulate confessions of faith with the following understanding, namely:

1963

constituted begs leave to present its report as follows:

Throughout its work your committee has been conscious of the contribution made by the statement of "The Southern Baptist Faith and Message" adopted by the Southern Baptist Convention in 1925. It quotes with approval its affirmation that "Christianity is supernatural in its origin and history. We repudiate every theory of religion which denies the supernatural elements in our faith."

Furthermore, it concurs in the introductory "statement of the historic Baptist conception of the nature and function of confessions of faith in our religious and denominational life . . . ." It is, therefore, quoted in full as a part of this report to the Convention:

2000

Our confessions of faith are rooted in historical precedent, as the church in every age has been called upon to define and defend its beliefs. Each generation of Christians bears the responsibility of guarding the treasury of truth that has been entrusted to us [2 Timothy 1:14]. Facing a new century, Southern Baptists must meet the demands and duties of the present hour.

New challenges to faith appear in every age. A pervasive anti-supernaturalism in the culture was answered by Southern Baptists in 1925, when the *Baptist Faith and Message* was first adopted by this Convention. In 1963, Southern Baptists responded to assaults upon the authority and truthfulness of the Bible by adopting revisions to the *Baptist Faith and Message*. The Convention added an article on "The Family" in 1998, thus answering cultural confusion with the clear teachings of Scripture. Now, faced with a culture hostile to the very notion of truth, this generation of Baptists must claim anew

1925	1963	2000

| | | the eternal truths of the Christian faith. |

the eternal truths of the Christian faith.

Your committee respects and celebrates the heritage of the *Baptist Faith and Message,* and affirms the decision of the Convention in 1925 to adopt the *New Hampshire Confession of Faith,* "revised at certain points and with some additional articles growing out of certain needs . . . ." We also respect the important contributions of the 1925 and 1963 editions of the *Baptist Faith and Message.*

With the 1963 committee, we have been guided in our work by the 1925 "statement of the historic Baptist conception of the nature and function of confessions of faith in our religious and denominational life . . . ." It is, therefore, quoted in full as a part of this report to the Convention:

1. That they constitute a consensus of opinion of some Baptist body, large or small, for the general instruction and guidance of our own people and others concerning those articles of the Christian faith which are most surely held among us. They are not intended

1. "That they constitute a consensus of opinion of some Baptist body, large or small, for the general instruction and guidance of our own people and others concerning those articles of the Christian faith which are most surely held among us. They are not intended

1. That they constitute a consensus of opinion of some Baptist body, large or small, for the general instruction and guidance of our own people and others concerning those articles of the Christian faith which are most surely held among us. They are not intended

1925	1963	2000
to add anything to the simple conditions of salvation revealed in the New Testament, viz., repentance towards God and faith in Jesus Christ as Saviour and Lord.	to add anything to the simple conditions of salvation revealed in the New Testament, viz., repentance towards God and faith in Jesus Christ as Savior and Lord.	to add anything to the simple conditions of salvation revealed in the New Testament, viz., repentance toward God and faith in Jesus Christ as Saviour and Lord.
2. That we do not regard them as complete statements of our faith, having any quality of finality or infallibility. As in the past so in the future, Baptists should hold themselves free to revise their statements of faith as may seem to them wise and expedient at any time.	2. "That we do not regard them as complete statements of our faith, having any quality of finality or infallibility. As in the past so in the future, Baptists should hold themselves free to revise their statements of faith as may seem to them wise and expedient at any time.	2. That we do not regard them as complete statements of our faith, having any quality of finality or infallibility. As in the past so in the future, Baptists should hold themselves free to revise their statements of faith as may seem to them wise and expedient at any time.
3. That any group of Baptists, large or small, have the inherent right to draw up for them- selves and publish to the world a confession of their faith whenever they may think it advisable to do so.	3. "That any group of Baptists, large or small, have the inherent right to draw up for them- selves and publish to the world a confession of their faith whenever they may think it advisable to do so.	3. That any group of Baptists, large or small, have the inherent right to draw up for them- selves and publish to the world a confession of their faith whenever they may think it advisable to do so.
4. That the sole authori- ty for faith and practice among Baptists is the Scriptures of the Old and New Testaments. Confessions are only guides in interpretation, having no authority over the conscience.	4. "That the sole author- ity for faith and practice among Baptists is the Scriptures of the Old and New Testaments. Confessions are only guides in interpretation, having no authority over the conscience.	4. That the sole authori- ty for faith and practice among Baptists is the Scriptures of the Old and New Testaments. Confessions are only guides in interpretation, having no authority over the conscience.
5. That they are statements of religious convictions, drawn from the Scriptures, and are	5. "That they are statements of religious convictions, drawn from the Scriptures, and are	5. That they are statements of religious convictions, drawn from the Scriptures, and are

1925	1963	2000

not to be used to hamper freedom of thought or investigation in other realms of life.

not to be used to hamper freedom of thought or investigation in other realms of life."

The 1925 Statement recommended "the New Hampshire Confession of Faith, revised at certain points, and with some additional articles growing out of certain needs . . . ." Your present committee has adopted the same pattern. It has sought to build upon the structure of the 1925 Statement, keeping in mind the "certain needs" of our generation. At times it has reproduced sections of that Statement without change. In other instances it has substituted words for clarity or added sentences for emphasis. At certain points it has combined articles, with minor changes in wording, to endeavor to relate certain doctrines to each other. In still others — e.g., "God" and "Salvation" — it has sought to bring together certain truths contained throughout the 1925 Statement in order to relate them more clearly and concisely. In no case has it sought to delete from or to add to the basic contents of the 1925 Statement.

not to be used to hamper freedom of thought or investigation in other realms of life.

Baptists cherish and defend religious liberty, and deny the right of any secular or religious authority to impose a confession of faith upon a church or body of churches. We honor the principles of soul competency and the priesthood of believers, affirming together both our liberty in Christ and our accountability to each other under the Word of God.

Baptist churches, associations, and general bodies have adopted confessions of faith as a witness to the world, and as instruments of doctrinal accountability. We are not embarrassed to state before the world that these are doctrines we hold precious and as essential to the Baptist tradition of faith and practice.

As a committee, we have been charged to address the "certain needs" of our own generation. In an age increasingly hostile to Christian truth, our challenge is to express the truth as re-

1925	1963	2000

Baptists are a people who profess a living faith. This faith is rooted and grounded in Jesus Christ who is "the same yesterday, and today, and forever." Therefore, the sole authority for faith and practice among Baptists is Jesus Christ whose will is revealed in the Holy Scriptures.

A living faith must experience a growing understanding of truth and must be continually interpreted and related to the needs of each new generation. Throughout their history Baptist bodies, both large and small, have issued statements of faith which comprise a consensus of their beliefs. Such statements have never been regarded as complete, infallible statements of faith, nor as official creeds carrying mandatory authority. Thus this generation of Southern Baptists is in historic succession of intent and purpose as it endeavors to state for its time and theological climate those articles of the Christian faith which are most surely held among us.

Baptists emphasize the soul's competency before

vealed in Scripture, and to bear witness to Jesus Christ, who is "*the Way, the Truth, and the Life.*"

The 1963 committee rightly sought to identify and affirm "certain definite doctrines that Baptists believe, cherish, and with which they have been and are now closely identified." Our living faith is established upon eternal truths. "Thus this generation of Southern Baptists is in historic succession of intent and purpose as it endeavors to state for its time and theological climate those articles of the Christian faith which are most surely held among us."

It is the purpose of this statement of faith and message to set forth certain teachings which we believe.

Respectfully Submitted,

The Baptist Faith and Message Study Committee
Adrian Rogers,
Chairman

| 1925 | 1963 | 2000 |

God, freedom in religion,
and the priesthood of the
believer. However, this
emphasis should not be
interpreted to mean that
there is an absence of
certain definite doctrines
that Baptists believe,
cherish, and with which
they have been and are
now closely identified.

It is the purpose of this
statement of faith and
message to set forth
certain teachings which
we believe.

Article I: The Scriptures

1925	1963	2000

We believe that the Holy Bible was written by men divinely inspired, and is a perfect treasure of heavenly instruction; that it has God for its author, salvation for its end, and truth, without any mixture of error, for its matter; that it reveals the principles by which God will judge us; and therefore is, and will remain to the end of the world, the true center of Christian union, and the supreme standard by which all human conduct, creeds and religious opinions should be tried.

The Holy Bible was written by men divinely inspired and is the record of God's revelation of Himself to man. It is a perfect treasure of divine instruction. It has God for its author, salvation for its end, and truth, without any mixture of error, for its matter. It reveals the principles by which God judges us; and therefore is, and will remain to the end of the world, the true center of Christian union, and the supreme standard by which all human conduct, creeds, and religious opinions should be tried. The criterion by which the Bible is to be interpreted is Jesus Christ.

The Holy Bible was written by men divinely inspired and is God's revelation of Himself to man. It is a perfect treasure of divine instruction. It has God for its author, salvation for its end, and truth, without any mixture of error, for its matter. Therefore, all Scripture is totally true and trustworthy. It reveals the principles by which God judges us, and therefore is, and will remain to the end of the world, the true center of Christian union, and the supreme standard by which all human conduct, creeds, and religious opinions should be tried. All Scripture is a testimony to Christ, who is Himself the focus of divine revelation.

Luke 16:29-31; 2 Tim. 3:15-17; Eph. 2:20; Heb. 1:1; 2 Peter 1:19-21; John 16:13-15; Matt. 22:29-31; Psalm 19:7-10; Psalm 119:1-8.

Ex. 24:4; Deut. 4:1-2; 17:19; Josh. 8:34; Psalms 19:7-10; 119:11,89,105,140; Isa. 34:16; 40:8; Jer. 15:16; 36; Matt. 5:17-18; 22:29; Luke 21:33; 24:44-46; John 5:39; 16:13-15; 17:17; Acts 2:16ff.; 17:11; Rom. 15:4; 16:25-26; 2 Tim. 3:15-17; Heb. 1:1-2; 4:12; 1 Peter 1:25; 2 Peter 1:19-21.

Exodus 24:4; Deuteronomy 4:1-2; 17:19; Joshua 8:34; Psalms 19:7-10; 119:11,89,105,140; Isaiah 34:16; 40:8; Jeremiah 15:16; 36:1-32; Matthew 5:17-18; 22:29; Luke 21:33; 24:44-46; John 5:39; 16:13-15; 17:17; Acts 2:16ff.; 17:11; Romans 15:4; 16:25-26; 2 Timothy 3:15-17; Hebrews 1:1-2; 4:12; 1 Peter 1:25; 2 Peter 1:19-21.

Article II: God

1925	1963	2000

There is one and only one living and true God, an intelligent, spiritual, and personal Being, the Creator, Preserver, and Ruler of the universe, infinite in holiness and all other perfections, to whom we owe the highest love, reverence, and obedience. He is revealed to us as Father, Son, and Holy Spirit, each with distinct personal attributes, but without division of nature, essence, or being.

Gen. 1:1; 1 Cor. 8:4-6; Deut. 6:4; Jer. 10:10; Isa. 48:12; Deut. 5:7; Ex. 3:14; Heb. 11:6; John 5:26; 1 Tim. 1:17; John 1:14-18; John 15:26; Gal. 4:6; Matt. 28:19.

There is one and only one living and true God. He is an intelligent, spiritual, and personal Being, the Creator, Redeemer, Preserver, and Ruler of the universe. God is infinite in holiness and all other perfections. To him we owe the highest love, reverence, and obedience. The eternal God reveals Himself to us as Father, Son, and Holy Spirit, with distinct personal attributes, but without division of nature, essence, or being.

1. God the Father
God as Father reigns with providential care over His universe, His creatures, and the flow of the stream of human history according to the purposes of His grace. He is all powerful, all loving, and all wise. God is Father in truth to those who become children of God through faith in Jesus Christ. He is fatherly in his attitude

---

There is one and only one living and true God. He is an intelligent, spiritual, and personal Being, the Creator, Redeemer, Preserver, and Ruler of the universe. God is infinite in holiness and all other perfections. God is all powerful and all knowing; and His perfect knowledge extends to all things, past, present, and future, including the future decisions of His free creatures. To Him we owe the highest love, reverence, and obedience. The eternal triune God reveals Himself to us as Father, Son, and Holy Spirit, with distinct personal attributes, but without division of nature, essence, or being.

A. God the Father
God as Father reigns with providential care over His universe, His creatures, and the flow of the stream of human history according to the purposes of His grace. He is all powerful, all knowing, all loving, and all wise. God is Father in truth to those who become children of God through faith in Jesus Christ. He is fatherly in

1925	1963	2000

1963

toward all men.
*Gen. 1:1; 2:7; Ex. 3:14;
6:2-3; 15:11ff.; 20:1ff.;
Levit. 22:2; Deut. 6:4;
32:6; 1 Chron. 29:10;
Psalm 19:1-3; Isa.
43:3,15; 64:8; Jer. 10:10;
17:13; Matt. 6:9ff.;
7:11; 23:9; 28:19; Mark
1:9-11; John 4:24; 5:26;
14:6-13; 17:1-8; Acts
1:7; Rom. 8:14-15; 1 Cor.
8:6; Gal. 4:6; Ephes. 4:6;
Col. 1:15; 1 Tim. 1:17;
Heb. 11:6; 12:9; 1 Peter
1:17; 1 John 5:7.*

2. God the Son
Christ is the eternal Son
of God. In His incarna-
tion as Jesus Christ He
was conceived of the
Holy Spirit and born of
the virgin Mary. Jesus
perfectly revealed and
did the will of God,
taking upon Himself the
demands and necessities
of human nature and
identifying Himself com-
pletely with mankind yet
without sin. He honored
the divine law by His
personal obedience,
and in His death on the
cross He made provision
for the redemption of
men from sin. He was
raised from the dead
with a glorified body and
appeared to His disciples

2000

His attitude toward all
men.
*Genesis 1:1; 2:7; Exodus
3:14; 6:2-3; 15:11ff.;
20:1ff.; Leviticus 22:2;
Deuteronomy 6:4; 32:6;
1 Chronicles 29:10;
Psalm 19:1-3; Isaiah
43:3,15; 64:8; Jeremiah
10:10; 17:13; Matthew
6:9ff.; 7:11; 23:9; 28:19;
Mark 1:9-11; John 4:24;
5:26; 14:6-13; 17:1-8;
Acts 1:7; Romans 8:14-
15; 1 Corinthians 8:6;
Galatians 4:6; Ephesians
4:6; Colossians 1:15; 1
Timothy 1:17; Hebrews
11:6; 12:9; 1 Peter 1:17;
1 John 5:7.*

B. God the Son
Christ is the eternal Son
of God. In His incarna-
tion as Jesus Christ He
was conceived of the
Holy Spirit and born of
the virgin Mary. Jesus
perfectly revealed and
did the will of God, tak-
ing upon Himself human
nature with its demands
and necessities and
identifying Himself com-
pletely with mankind yet
without sin. He honored
the divine law by His
personal obedience, and
in His substitutionary
death on the cross He
made provision for the
redemption of men from
sin. He was raised from
the dead with a glorified
body and appeared to

1925	1963	2000

1963 column:

as the person who was with them before His crucifixion. He ascended into heaven and is now exalted at the right hand of God where He is the One Mediator, partaking of the nature of God and of man, and in whose Person is effected the reconciliation between God and man. He will return in power and glory to judge the world and to consummate His redemptive mission. He now dwells in all believers as the living and ever present Lord.

Gen. 18:1ff.; Psalms 2:7ff.; 110:1ff.; Isa. 7:14; 53; Matt. 1:18-23; 3:17; 8:29; 11:27; 14:33; 16:16,27; 17:5; 27; 28:1-6,19; Mark 1:1; 3:11; Luke 1:35; 4:41; 22:70; 24:46; John 1:1-18,29; 10:30,38; 11:25-27; 12:44-50; 14:7-11; 16:15-16,28; 17:1-5, 21-22; 20:1-20,28; Acts 1:9; 2:22-24; 7:55-56; 9:4-5,20; Rom. 1:3-4; 3:23-26; 5:6-21; 8:1-3,34; 10:4; 1 Cor. 1:30; 2:2; 8:6; 15:1-8,24-28; 2 Cor. 5:19-21; 8:9; Gal. 4:4-5; Ephes. 1:20; 3:11; 4:7-10; Phil. 2:5-11; Col. 1:13-22; 2:9; 1 Thess. 4:14-18; 1 Tim. 2:5-6; 3:16; Titus 2:13-14; Heb. 1:1-3; 4:14-15; 7:14-28; 9:12-15,24-28; 12:2;

2000 column:

His disciples as the person who was with them before His crucifixion. He ascended into heaven and is now exalted at the right hand of God where He is the One Mediator, fully God, fully man, in whose Person is effected the reconciliation between God and man. He will return in power and glory to judge the world and to consummate His redemptive mission. He now dwells in all believers as the living and ever present Lord.

Genesis 18:1ff.; Psalms 2:7ff.; 110:1ff.; Isaiah 7:14; 53; Matthew 1:18-23; 3:17; 8:29; 11:27; 14:33; 16:16,27; 17:5; 27; 28:1-6,19; Mark 1:1; 3:11; Luke 1:35; 4:41; 22:70; 24:46; John 1:1-18,29; 10:30,38; 11:25-27; 12:44-50; 14:7-11; 16:15-16,28; 17:1-5, 21-22; 20:1-20,28; Acts 1:9; 2:22-24; 7:55-56; 9:4-5,20; Romans 1:3-4; 3:23-26; 5:6-21; 8:1-3,34; 10:4; 1 Corinthians 1:30; 2:2; 8:6; 15:1-8,24-28; 2 Corinthians 5:19-21; 8:9; Galatians 4:4-5; Ephesians 1:20; 3:11; 4:7-10; Philippians 2:5-11; Colossians 1:13-22; 2:9; 1 Thessalonians 4:14-18; 1 Timothy 2:5-6; 3:16; Titus 2:13-14;

1925	1963	2000

1925

13:8; 1 Peter 2:21-25;
3:22; 1 John 1:7-9; 3:2;
4:14-15; 5:9; 2 John 7-9;
Rev. 1:13-16; 5:9-14;
12:10-11; 13:8; 19:16.

1963

Hebrews 1:1-3; 4:14-15;
7:14-28; 9:12-15,24-28;
12:2; 13:8; 1 Peter 2:21-
25; 3:22; 1 John 1:7-9;
3:2; 4:14-15; 5:9; 2 John
7-9; Revelation 1:13-16;
5:9-14; 12:10-11; 13:8;
19:16.

3. God the Holy Spirit
The Holy Spirit is
the Spirit of God. He
inspired holy men of old
to write the Scriptures.
Through illumination
He enables men to un-
derstand truth. He exalts
Christ. He convicts of
sin, of righteousness and
of judgment. He calls
men to the Saviour, and
effects regeneration.
He cultivates Christian
character, comforts be-
lievers, and bestows the
spiritual gifts by which
they serve God through
His church. He seals the
believer unto the day of
final redemption. His
presence in the Chris-
tian is the assurance of
God to bring the believer
into the fulness of the
stature of Christ. He
enlightens and empow-
ers the believer and the
church in worship, evan-
gelism, and service.

C. God the Holy Spirit
The Holy Spirit is the
Spirit of God, fully
divine. He inspired holy
men of old to write the
Scriptures. Through
illumination He enables
men to understand
truth. He exalts Christ.
He convicts men of sin,
of righteousness, and
of judgment. He calls
men to the Saviour, and
effects regeneration. At
the moment of regener-
ation He baptizes every
believer into the Body
of Christ. He cultivates
Christian character,
comforts believers, and
bestows the spiritual
gifts by which they
serve God through His
church. He seals the
believer unto the day of
final redemption. His
presence in the Chris-
tian is the guarantee
that God will bring the
believer into the fullness
of the stature of Christ.
He enlightens and em-
powers the believer and
the church in worship,
evangelism, and service.

1925	1963	2000

| | *Gen.* 1:2; *Judg.* 14:6; *Job* 26:13; *Psalms* 51:11; 139:7ff.; *Isa.* 61:1-3; *Joel* 2:28-32; *Matt.* 1:18; 3:16; 4:1; 12:28-32; 28:19; *Mark* 1:10,12; *Luke* 1:35; 4:1,18-19; 11:13; 12:12; 24:49; *John* 4:24; 14:16-17,26; 15:26; 16:7-14; *Acts* 1:8; 2:1-4,38; 4:31; 5:3; 6:3; 7:55; 8:17,39; 10:44; 13:2; 15:28; 16:6; 19:1-6; *Rom.* 8:9-11,14-16,26-27; 1 *Cor.* 2:10-14; 3:16; 12:3-11; *Gal.* 4:6; *Ephes.* 1:13-14; 4:30; 5:18; 1 *Thess.* 5:19; 1 *Tim.* 3:16; 4:1; 2 *Tim.* 1:14; 3:16; *Heb.* 9:8,14; 2 *Peter* 1:21; 1 *John* 4:13; 5:6-7; *Rev.* 1:10; 22:17. | *Genesis* 1:2; *Judges* 14:6; *Job* 26:13; *Psalms* 51:11; 139:7ff.; *Isaiah* 61:1-3; *Joel* 2:28-32; *Matthew* 1:18; 3:16; 4:1; 12:28-32; 28:19; *Mark* 1:10,12; *Luke* 1:35; 4:1,18-19; 11:13; 12:12; 24:49; *John* 4:24; 14:16-17,26; 15:26; 16:7-14; *Acts* 1:8; 2:1-4,38; 4:31; 5:3; 6:3; 7:55; 8:17,39; 10:44; 13:2; 15:28; 16:6; 19:1-6; *Romans* 8:9-11,14-16,26-27; 1 *Corinthians* 2:10-14; 3:16; 12:3-11,13; *Galatians* 4:6; *Ephesians* 1:13-14; 4:30; 5:18; 1 *Thessalonians* 5:19; 1 *Timothy* 3:16; 4:1; 2 *Timothy* 1:14; 3:16; *Hebrews* 9:8,14; 2 *Peter* 1:21; 1 *John* 4:13; 5:6-7; *Revelation* 1:10; 22:17. |

Article III: Man

1925	1963	2000
Man was created by the special act of God, as recorded in Genesis. "So God created man in his own image, in the image of God created he him; male and female created he them" (Gen. 1:27). "And the Lord God formed man of the dust of the ground, and breathed into his nostrils the breath of life; and man became a living soul" (Gen. 2:7). He was created in a state of holiness under the law of his Maker, but, through the temptation of Satan, he transgressed the command of God and fell from his original holiness and righteousness; whereby his posterity inherit a nature corrupt and in bondage to sin, are under condemnation, and as soon as they are capable of moral action, become actual transgressors.	Man was created by the special act of God, in His own image, and is the crowning work of His creation. In the beginning man was innocent of sin and was endowed by his Creator with freedom of choice. By his free choice man sinned against God and brought sin into the human race. Through the temptation of Satan man transgressed the command of God, and fell from his original innocence; whereby his posterity inherit a nature and an environment inclined toward sin, and as soon as they are capable of moral action become transgressors and are under condemnation. Only the grace of God can bring man into His holy fellowship and enable man to fulfil the creative purpose of God. The sacredness of human personality is evident in that God created man in His own image, and in that Christ died for man; therefore every man possesses dignity and is worthy of respect and Christian love.	Man is the special creation of God, made in His own image. He created them male and female as the crowning work of His creation. The gift of gender is thus part of the goodness of God's creation. In the beginning man was innocent of sin and was endowed by his Creator with freedom of choice. By his free choice man sinned against God and brought sin into the human race. Through the temptation of Satan man transgressed the command of God, and fell from his original innocence whereby his posterity inherit a nature and an environment inclined toward sin. Therefore, as soon as they are capable of moral action, they become transgressors and are under condemnation. Only the grace of God can bring man into His holy fellowship and enable man to fulfill the creative purpose of God. The sacredness of human personality is evident in that God created man in His own image, and in that Christ died for man; therefore, every person of every

1925	1963	2000
		race possesses full dignity and is worthy of respect and Christian love.
Gen. 1:27; Gen. 2:7; John 1:23; Gen. 3:4-7; Gen. 3:22-24; Rom. 5:12,14,19, 21; Rom. 7:23-25; Rom. 11:18,22,32-33; Col. 1:21.

Note: Article III was titled "The Fall of Man" in the 1925 BF&M. | Gen. 1:26-30; 2:5,7,18-22; 3; 9:6; Psalms 1; 8:3-6; 32:1-5; 51:5; Isa. 6:5; Jer. 17:5; Matt. 16:26; Acts 17:26-31; Rom. 1:19-32; 3:10-18,23; 5:6,12,19; 6:6; 7:14-25; 8:14-18,29; 1 Cor. 1:21-31; 15:19,21-22; Eph. 2:1-22; Col. 1:21-22; 3:9-11. | Genesis 1:26-30; 2:5,7,18-22; 3; 9:6; Psalms 1; 8:3-6; 32:1-5; 51:5; Isaiah 6:5; Jeremiah 17:5; Matthew 16:26; Acts 17:26-31; Romans 1:19-32; 3:10-18,23; 5:6,12,19; 6:6; 7:14-25; 8:14-18,29; 1 Corinthians 1:21-31; 15:19,21-22; Ephesians 2:1-22; Colossians 1:21-22; 3:9-11. |

Article IV: Salvation

1925	1963	2000

IV. The Way of Salvation

The salvation of sinners is wholly of grace, through the mediatorial office of the Son of God, who by the Holy Spirit was born of the Virgin Mary and took upon him our nature, yet without sin; honored the divine law by his personal obedience and made atonement for our sins by his death. Being risen from the dead, he is now enthroned in Heaven, and, uniting in his person the tenderest sympathies with divine perfections, he is in every way qualified to be a compassionate and all-sufficient Saviour.

Col. 1:21-22; Eph. 1:7-10; Gal. 2:19-20; Gal. 3:13; Rom. 1:4; Eph. 1:20-23; Matt. 1:21-25; Luke 1:35; 2:11; Rom. 3:25.

V. Justification

Justification is God's gracious and full acquittal upon principles of righteousness of all sinners who believe in Christ. This blessing is bestowed, not in consid-

Salvation involves the redemption of the whole man, and is offered freely to all who accept Jesus Christ as Lord and Saviour, who by His own blood obtained eternal redemption for the believer. In its broadest sense salvation includes regeneration, sanctification, and glorification.

1. Regeneration, or the new birth, is a work of God's grace whereby believers become new creatures in Christ Jesus. It is a change of heart wrought by the Holy Spirit through conviction of sin, to which the sinner responds in repentance toward God and faith in the Lord Jesus Christ.

Repentance and faith are inseparable experiences of grace. Repentance is a genuine turning from sin toward God. Faith is the acceptance of Jesus Christ and commitment of the entire personality to Him as Lord and Saviour. Justification is God's gracious and full

Salvation involves the redemption of the whole man, and is offered freely to all who accept Jesus Christ as Lord and Saviour, who by His own blood obtained eternal redemption for the believer. In its broadest sense salvation includes regeneration, justification, sanctification, and glorification. There is no salvation apart from personal faith in Jesus Christ as Lord.

A. Regeneration, or the new birth, is a work of God's grace whereby believers become new creatures in Christ Jesus. It is a change of heart wrought by the Holy Spirit through conviction of sin, to which the sinner responds in repentance toward God and faith in the Lord Jesus Christ. Repentance and faith are inseparable experiences of grace.

Repentance is a genuine turning from sin toward God. Faith is the acceptance of Jesus Christ and commitment of the entire personality to Him as Lord and Saviour.

B. Justification is God's gracious and full

1925	1963	2000

eration of any works of righteousness which we have done, but through the redemption that is in and through Jesus Christ. It brings us into a state of most blessed peace and favor with God, and secures every other needed blessing.

Rom. 3:24; 4:2; 5:1-2; 8:30; *Eph.* 1:7; 1 *Cor.* 1:30-31; 2 *Cor.* 5:21.

VI. The Freeness of Salvation

The blessings of salvation are made free to all by the gospel. It is the duty of all to accept them by penitent and obedient faith. Nothing prevents the salvation of the greatest sinner except his own voluntary refusal to accept Jesus Christ as teacher, Saviour, and Lord.

Eph. 1:5; 2:4-10; 1 *Cor.* 1:30-31; *Rom.* 5:1-9; *Rev.* 22:17; *John* 3:16; *Mark* 16:16.

VII. Regeneration

Regeneration or the new birth is a change of heart wrought by the Holy Spirit, whereby we become partakers of the divine nature and a holy disposition is given, lead-

acquittal upon principles of His righteousness of all sinners who repent and believe in Christ. Justification brings the believer into a relationship of peace and favor with God.

2. Sanctification is the experience, beginning in regeneration, by which the believer is set apart to God's purposes, and is enabled to progress toward moral and spiritual perfection through the presence and power of the Holy Spirit dwelling in him. Growth in grace should continue throughout the regenerate person's life.

3. Glorification is the culmination of salvation and is the final blessed and abiding state of the redeemed.

Gen. 3:15; *Ex.* 3:14-17; 6:2-8; *Matt.* 1:21; 4:17; 16:21-26; 27:22-28:6; *Luke* 1:68-69; 2:28-32; *John* 1:11-14,29; 3:3-21,36; 5:24; 10:9,28-29; 15:1-16; 17:17; *Acts* 2:21; 4:12; 15:11; 16:30-31; 17:30-31; 20:32; *Rom.* 1:16-18; 2:4; 3:23-25; 4:3ff.; 5:8-10; 6:1-23; 8:1-18,29-39; 10:9-10,13; 13:11-14; 1 *Cor.* 1:18,30; 6:19-20;

acquittal upon principles of His righteousness of all sinners who repent and believe in Christ. Justification brings the believer unto a relationship of peace and favor with God.

C. Sanctification is the experience, beginning in regeneration, by which the believer is set apart to God's purposes, and is enabled to progress toward moral and spiritual maturity through the presence and power of the Holy Spirit dwelling in him. Growth in grace should continue throughout the regenerate person's life.

D. Glorification is the culmination of salvation and is the final blessed and abiding state of the redeemed.

Genesis 3:15; *Exodus* 3:14-17; 6:2-8; *Matthew* 1:21; 4:17; 16:21-26; 27:22-28:6; *Luke* 1:68-69; 2:28-32; *John* 1:11-14,29; 3:3-21,36; 5:24; 10:9,28-29; 15:1-16; 17:17; *Acts* 2:21; 4:12; 15:11; 16:30-31; 17:30-31; 20:32; *Romans* 1:16-18; 2:4; 3:23-25; 4:3ff.; 5:8-10; 6:1-23; 8:1-18,29-39; 10:9-10,13; 13:11-14; 1 *Corinthians*

1925	1963	2000

ing to the love and prac-
tice of righteousness. It
is a work of God's free
grace conditioned upon
faith in Christ and made
manifest by the fruit
which we bring forth to
the glory of God.

John 3:1-8, 1:16-18;
Rom. 8:2; Eph. 2:1,5-
6,8,10; Eph. 4:30,32;
Col. 3:1-11; Titus 3:5.

VIII. Repentance and
Faith

We believe that
repentance and faith
are sacred duties, and
also inseparable graces,
wrought in our souls by
the regenerating Spirit
of God; whereby being
deeply convinced of our
guilt, danger, and help-
lessness, and of the way
of salvation by Christ,
we turn to God with un-
feigned contrition, con-
fession, and supplication
for mercy; at the same
time heartily receiving
the Lord Jesus Christ as
our Prophet, Priest, and
King, and relying on him
alone as the only and
all-sufficient Saviour.

Luke 22:31-34; Mark
1:15; 1 Tim. 1:13;
Rom. 3:25,27,31; Rom.
4:3,9,12,16-17; John
16:8-11.

15:10; 2 Cor. 5:17-20;
Gal. 2:20; 3:13; 5:22-25;
6:15; Ephes. 1:7; 2:8-22;
4:11-16; Phil. 2:12-13;
Col. 1:9-22; 3:1ff.; 1
Thess. 5:23-24; 2 Tim.
1:12; Titus 2:11-14; Heb.
2:1-3; 5:8-9; 9:24-28;
11:1-12:8,14; James
2:14-26; 1 Peter 1:2-23;
1 John 1:6-2:11; Rev.
3:20; 21:1-22:5.

1:18,30; 6:19-20; 15:10;
2 Corinthians 5:17-20;
Galatians 2:20; 3:13;
5:22-25; 6:15; Ephesians
1:7; 2:8-22; 4:11-16;
Philippians 2:12-13;
Colossians 1:9-22; 3:1ff.;
1 Thessalonians 5:23-24;
2 Timothy 1:12; Titus
2:11-14; Hebrews 2:1-3;
5:8-9; 9:24-28; 11:1-
12:8,14; James 2:14-26;
1 Peter 1:2-23; 1 John
1:6-2:11; Revelation
3:20; 21:1-22:5.

1925	1963	2000

[See the next table (God's
Purpose of Grace) for
Article IX from the
1925 BF&M – God's
Purpose of Grace.]

X. Sanctification

Sanctification is the
process by which the
regenerate gradually
attain to moral and spir-
itual perfection through
the presence and power
of the Holy Spirit
dwelling in their hearts.
It continues throughout
the earthly life, and is
accomplished by the use
of all the ordinary means
of grace, and particularly
by the Word of God.

Acts 20:32; John 17:17;
Rom. 6:5-6; Eph. 3:16;
Rom. 4:14; Gal. 5:24;
Heb. 12:14; Rom. 7:18-
25; 2 Cor. 3:18; Gal.
5:16,25-26.

[See the next table (God's
Purpose of Grace) for
Article XI of the 1925
BF&M: Perseverance.]

Article V: God's Purpose of Grace

1925	1963	2000

IX. God's Purpose of Grace

Election is the gracious purpose of God, according to which he regenerates, sanctifies and saves sinners. It is perfectly consistent with the free agency of man, and comprehends all the means in connection with the end. It is a most glorious display of God's sovereign goodness, and is infinitely wise, holy, and unchangeable. It excludes boasting and promotes humility. It encourages the use of means in the highest degree.

Rom. 8:30; 11:7; Eph. 1:10; Acts 26:18; Eph. 1:17-19; 2 Tim. 1:9; Psalm 110:3; 1 Cor. 2:14; Eph. 2:5; John 6:44-45,65; Rom. 10:12-15.

XI. Perseverance

All real believers endure to the end. Their continuance in well-doing is the mark which distinguishes them from mere professors. A special Providence cares for them, and they are kept by the power of God through faith unto salvation.

Election is the gracious purpose of God, according to which He regenerates, sanctifies, and glorifies sinners. It is consistent with the free agency of man and comprehends all the means in connection with the end. It is a glorious display of God's sovereign goodness, and is infinitely wise, holy, and unchangeable. It excludes boasting and promotes humility.

All true believers endure to the end. Those whom God has accepted in Christ, and sanctified by His Spirit, will never fall away from the state of grace, but shall persevere to the end. Believers may fall into sin through neglect and temptation,

Election is the gracious purpose of God, according to which He regenerates, justifies, sanctifies, and glorifies sinners. It is consistent with the free agency of man, and comprehends all the means in connection with the end. It is the glorious display of God's sovereign goodness, and is infinitely wise, holy, and unchangeable. It excludes boasting and promotes humility.

All true believers endure to the end. Those whom God has accepted in Christ, and sanctified by His Spirit, will never fall away from the state of grace, but shall persevere to the end. Believers may fall into sin through neglect and temptation,

1925	1963	2000
	whereby they grieve the Spirit, impair their graces and comforts, bring reproach on the cause of Christ, and temporal judgments on themselves, yet they shall be kept by the power of God through faith unto salvation.	whereby they grieve the Spirit, impair their graces and comforts, and bring reproach on the cause of Christ and temporal judgments on themselves; yet they shall be kept by the power of God through faith unto salvation.

John 10:28-29; 2 *Tim.* 2:19; 1 *John* 2:19; 1 *Cor.* 11:32; *Rom.* 8:30; 9:11,16; *Rom.* 5:9-10; *Matt.* 26:70-75.

Gen. 12:1-3; *Ex.* 19:5-8; 1 *Sam.* 8:4-7,19-22; *Isa.* 5:1-7; *Jer.* 31:31ff.; *Matt.* 16:18-19; 21:28-45; 24:22,31; 25:34; *Luke* 1:68-79; 2:29-32; 19:41-44; 24:44-48; *John* 1:12-14; 3:16; 5:24; 6:44-45,65; 10:27-29; 15:16; 17:6,12,17-18; *Acts* 20:32; *Rom.* 5:9-10; 8:28-39; 10:12-15; 11:5-7,26-36; 1 *Cor.* 1:1-2; 15:24-28; *Ephes.* 1:4-23; 2:1-10; 3:1-11; *Col.* 1:12-14; 2 *Thess.* 2:13-14; 2 *Tim.* 1:12; 2:10,19; *Heb.* 11:39-12:2; 1 *Peter* 1:2-5,13; 2:4-10; 1 *John* 1:7-9; 2:19; 3:2.

Genesis 12:1-3; *Exodus* 19:5-8; 1 *Samuel* 8:4-7,19-22; *Isaiah* 5:1-7; *Jeremiah* 31:31ff.; *Matthew* 16:18-19; 21:28-45; 24:22,31; 25:34; *Luke* 1:68-79; 2:29-32; 19:41-44; 24:44-48; *John* 1:12-14; 3:16; 5:24; 6:44-45,65; 10:27-29; 15:16; 17:6, 12, 17-18; *Acts* 20:32; *Romans* 5:9-10; 8:28-39; 10:12-15; 11:5-7,26-36; 1 *Corinthians* 1:1-2; 15:24-28; *Ephesians* 1:4-23; 2:1-10; 3:1-11; *Colossians* 1:12-14; 2 *Thessalonians* 2:13-14; 2 *Timothy* 1:12; 2:10,19; *Hebrews* 11:39-12:2; *James* 1:12; 1 *Peter* 1:2-5,13; 2:4-10; 1 *John* 1:7-9; 2:19; 3:2.

Article VI: The Church

1925	1963	2000

A church of Christ is a congregation of baptized believers, associated by covenant in the faith and fellowship of the gospel; observing the ordinances of Christ, governed by his laws, and exercising the gifts, rights, and privileges invested in them by his word, and seeking to extend the gospel to the ends of the earth. Its Scriptural officers are bishops, or elders, and deacons.

A New Testament church of the Lord Jesus Christ is a local body of baptized believers who are associated by covenant in the faith and fellowship of the gospel, observing the two ordinances of Christ, committed to His teachings, exercising the gifts, rights, and privileges invested in them by His Word, and seeking to extend the gospel to the ends of the earth.

This church is an autonomous body, operating through democratic processes under the Lordship of Jesus Christ. In such a congregation, members are equally responsible. Its Scriptural officers are pastors and deacons.

The New Testament speaks also of the church as the body of Christ which includes all of the redeemed of all the ages.

A New Testament church of the Lord Jesus Christ is an autonomous local congregation of baptized believers, associated by covenant in the faith and fellowship of the gospel; observing the two ordinances of Christ, governed by His laws, exercising the gifts, rights, and privileges invested in them by His Word, and seeking to extend the gospel to the ends of the earth. Each congregation operates under the Lordship of Christ through democratic processes. In such a congregation each member is responsible and accountable to Christ as Lord. Its scriptural officers are pastors and deacons. While both men and women are gifted for service in the church, the office of pastor is limited to men as qualified by Scripture.

The New Testament speaks also of the church as the Body of Christ which includes all of the redeemed of all the ages, believers from every tribe, and tongue, and people, and nation.

1925	1963	2000
Matt. 16:18; Matt. 18:15-18; Rom. 1:7; 1 Cor. 1:2; Acts 2:41-42; 5:13-14; 2 Cor. 9:13; Phil. 1:1; 1 Tim. 4:14; Acts 14:23; Acts 6:3,5-6; Heb. 13:17; 1 Cor. 9:6,14.	Matt. 16:15-19; 18:15-20; Acts 2:41-42,47; 5:11-14; 6:3-6; 13:1-3; 14:23,27; 15:1-30; 16:5; 20:28; Rom. 1:7; 1 Cor. 1:2; 3:16; 5:4-5; 7:17; 9:13-14; 2:19-22; 3:8-11,21; 5:22-32; Phil. 1:1; Col. 1:18; 1 Tim. 3:1-15; 4:14; 1 Peter 5:1-4; Rev. 2-3; 21:2-3.	Matthew 16:15-19; 18:15-20; Acts 2:41-42,47; 5:11-14; 6:3-6; 13:1-3; 14:23,27; 15:1-30; 16:5; 20:28; Romans 1:7; 1 Corinthians 1:2; 3:16; 5:4-5; 7:17; 9:13-14; 12; Ephesians 1:22-23; 2:19-22; 3:8-11,21; 5:22-32; Philippians 1:1; Colossians 1:18; 1 Timothy 2:9-14; 3:1-15; 4:14; Hebrews 11:39-40; 1 Peter 5:1-4; Revelation 2-3; 21:2-3.

Note: Article XII was titled "The Gospel Church" in the 1925 BF&M.

Article VII: Baptism and The Lord's Supper

1925	1963	2000

Christian baptism is the immersion of a believer in water in the name of the Father, the Son, and the Holy Spirit. The act is a symbol of our faith in a crucified, buried and risen Saviour. It is prerequisite to the privileges of a church relation and to the Lord's Supper, in which the members of the church, by the use of bread and wine, commemorate the dying love of Christ.

Matt. 28:19-20; 1 Cor. 4:1; Rom. 6:3-5; Col. 2:12; Mark 1:4; Matt. 3:16; John 3:23; 1 Cor. 11:23-26; 1 Cor. 10:16-17,21; Matt. 26:26-27; Acts 8:38-39; Mark 1:9-11.

Note: Article XIII was titled "Baptism and the Lord's Supper" in the 1925 BF&M.

Christian baptism is the immersion of a believer in water in the name of the Father, the Son, and the Holy Spirit. It is an act of obedience symbolizing the believer's faith in a crucified, buried, and risen Saviour, the believer's death to sin, the burial of the old life, and the resurrection to walk in newness of life in Christ Jesus. It is a testimony to his faith in the final resurrection of the dead. Being a church ordinance, it is prerequisite to the privileges of church membership and to the Lord's Supper.

The Lord's Supper is a symbolic act of obedience whereby members of the church, through partaking of the bread and the fruit of the vine, memorialize the death of the Redeemer and anticipate His second coming.

Matt. 3:13-17; 26:26-30; 28:19-20; Mark 1:9-11; 14:22-26; Luke 3:21-22; 22:19-20; John 3:23; Acts 2:41-42; 8:35-39; 16:30-33; Acts 20:7; Rom. 6:3-5; 1 Cor. 10:16,21; 11:23-29; Col. 2:12.

Christian baptism is the immersion of a believer in water in the name of the Father, the Son, and the Holy Spirit. It is an act of obedience symbolizing the believer's faith in a crucified, buried, and risen Saviour, the believer's death to sin, the burial of the old life, and the resurrection to walk in newness of life in Christ Jesus. It is a testimony to his faith in the final resurrection of the dead. Being a church ordinance, it is prerequisite to the privileges of church membership and to the Lord's Supper.

The Lord's Supper is a symbolic act of obedience whereby members of the church, through partaking of the bread and the fruit of the vine, memorialize the death of the Redeemer and anticipate His second coming.

Matthew 3:13-17; 26:26-30; 28:19-20; Mark 1:9-11; 14:22-26; Luke 3:21-22; 22:19-20; John 3:23; Acts 2:41-42; 8:35-39; 16:30-33; 20:7; Romans 6:3-5; 1 Corinthians 10:16,21; 11:23-29; Colossians 2:12.

Article VIII: The Lord's Day

1925	1963	2000
The first day of the week is the Lord's day. It is a Christian institution for regular observance. It commemorates the resurrection of Christ from the dead and should be employed in exercises of worship and spiritual devotion, both public and private, and by refraining from worldly amusements, and resting from secular employments, works of necessity and mercy only excepted.	The first day of the week is the Lord's Day. It is a Christian institution for regular observance. It commemorates the resurrection of Christ from the dead and should be employed in exercises of worship and spiritual devotion, both public and private, and by refraining from worldly amusements, and resting from secular employments, works of necessity and mercy only being excepted.	The first day of the week is the Lord's Day. It is a Christian institution for regular observance. It commemorates the resurrection of Christ from the dead and should include exercises of worship and spiritual devotion, both public and private. Activities on the Lord's Day should be commensurate with the Christian's conscience under the Lordship of Jesus Christ.
Ex. 20:3-6; Matt. 4:10; Matt. 28:19; 1 Tim. 4:13; Col. 3:16; John 4:21; Ex. 20:8; 1 Cor. 16:1-2; Acts 20:7; Rev. 1:1; Matt. 12:1-13. Note: *Article XIV was titled "The Lord's Day" in the 1925 BF&M.*	*Ex. 20:8-11; Matt. 12:1-12; 28:1ff.; Mark 2:27-28; 16:1-7; Luke 24:1-3,33-36; John 4:21-24; 20:1,19-28; Acts 20:7; 1 Cor. 16:1-2; Col. 2:16; 3:16; Rev. 1:10.*	*Exodus 20:8-11; Matthew 12:1-12; 28:1ff.; Mark 2:27-28; 16:1-7; Luke 24:1-3,33-36; John 4:21-24; 20:1,19-28; Acts 20:7; Romans 14:5-10; I Corinthians 16:1-2; Colossians 2:16; 3:16; Revelation 1:10.*

Article IX: The Kingdom

1925	1963	2000

The Kingdom of God is the reign of God in the heart and life of the individual in every human relationship, and in every form and institution of organized human society. The chief means for promoting the Kingdom of God on earth are preaching the gospel of Christ, and teaching the principles of righteousness contained therein. The Kingdom of God will be complete when every thought and will of man shall be brought into captivity to the will of Christ. And it is the duty of all Christ's people to pray and labor continually that his Kingdom may come and his will be done on earth as it is done in heaven.

Dan. 2:37-44; 7:18; Matt. 4:23; 8:12; 12:25; 13:38,43; 25:34; 26:29; Mark 11:10; Luke 12:32; 22:29; Acts 1:6; 1 Cor. 15:24; Col. 1:13; Heb. 12:28; Rev. 1:9; Luke 4:43; 8:1; 9:2; 17:20-21; John 3:3; John 18:36; Matt. 6:10; Luke 23:42.

Note: Article XXV was titled "The Kingdom" in the 1925 BF&M.

The kingdom of God includes both His general sovereignty over the universe and His particular kingship over men who willfully acknowledge Him as King. Particularly the kingdom is the realm of salvation into which men enter by trustful, childlike commitment to Jesus Christ. Christians ought to pray and to labor that the kingdom may come and God's will be done on earth. The full consummation of the kingdom awaits the return of Jesus Christ and the end of this age.

Gen. 1:1; Isa. 9:6-7; Jer. 23:5-6; Matt. 3:2; 4:8-10,23; 12:25-28; 13:1-52; 25:31-46; 26:29; Mark 1:14-15; 9:1; Luke 4:43; 8:1; 9:2; 12:31-32; 17:20-21; 23:42; John 3:3; 18:36; Acts 1:6-7; 17:22-31; Rom. 5:17; 8:19; 1 Cor. 15:24-28; Col. 1:13; Heb. 11:10,16; 12:28; 1 Peter 2:4-10; 4:13; Rev. 1:6,9; 5:10; 11:15; 21-22.

The Kingdom of God includes both His general sovereignty over the universe and His particular kingship over men who willfully acknowledge Him as King. Particularly the Kingdom is the realm of salvation into which men enter by trustful, childlike commitment to Jesus Christ. Christians ought to pray and to labor that the Kingdom may come and God's will be done on earth. The full consummation of the Kingdom awaits the return of Jesus Christ and the end of this age.

Genesis 1:1; Isaiah 9:6-7; Jeremiah 23:5-6; Matthew 3:2; 4:8-10,23; 12:25-28; 13:1-52; 25:31-46; 26:29; Mark 1:14-15; 9:1; Luke 4:43; 8:1; 9:2; 12:31-32; 17:20-21; 23:42; John 3:3; 18:36; Acts 1:6-7; 17:22-31; Romans 5:17; 8:19; 1 Corinthians 15:24-28; Colossians 1:13; Hebrews 11:10,16; 12:28; 1 Peter 2:4-10; 4:13; Revelation 1:6,9; 5:10; 11:15; 21-22.

Article X: Last Things

1925	1963	2000

XV. The Righteous and the Wicked

There is a radical and essential difference between the righteous and wicked. Those only who are justified through the name of the Lord Jesus Christ and sanctified by the Holy Spirit are truly righteous in his sight. Those who continue in impenitence and unbelief are in his sight wicked and are under condemnation. This distinction between the righteous and the wicked holds in and after death, and will be made manifest at the judgment when final and everlasting awards are made to all men.

Gen. 3:19; Acts 13:36; Luke 23:43; 2 Cor. 5:1, 6,8; Phil. 1:23; 1 Cor. 15:51-52; 1 Thess. 4:17; Phil. 3:21; 1 Cor. 6:3; Matt. 25:32-46; Rom. 9:22-23; Mark 9:48; 1 Thess. 1:7-10; Rev. 22:20.

XVI. The Resurrection

The Scriptures clearly teach that Jesus rose from the dead. His grave was emptied of its contents. He appeared to the disciples after his resurrec-

God, in His own time and in His own way, will bring the world to its appropriate end. According to His promise, Jesus Christ will return personally and visibly in glory to the earth; the dead will be raised; and Christ will judge all men in righteousness. The unrighteous will be consigned to hell, the place of everlasting punishment. The righteous in their resurrected and glorified bodies will receive their reward and will dwell forever in heaven with the Lord.

Isa. 2:4; 11:9; Matt. 16:27; 18:8-9; 19:28; 24:27,30,36,44; 25:31-46; 26:64; Mark 8:38; 9:43-48; Luke 12:40,48; 16:19-26; 17:22-37; 21:27-28; John 14:1-3; Acts 1:11; 17:31; Rom. 14:10; 1 Cor. 4:5; 15:24-28,35-58; 2 Cor. 5:10; Phil. 3:20-21; Col. 1:5; 3:4; 1 Thess. 4:14-18; 5:1ff.; 2 Thess. 1:7ff.; 2; 1 Tim. 6:14; 2 Tim. 4:1,8; Titus 2:13; Heb. 9:27-28; James 5:8; 2 Peter 3:7ff.; 1 John 2:28; 3:2; Jude 14; Rev. 1:18; 3:11; 20:1-22:13.

God, in His own time and in His own way, will bring the world to its appropriate end. According to His promise, Jesus Christ will return personally and visibly in glory to the earth; the dead will be raised; and Christ will judge all men in righteousness. The unrighteous will be consigned to Hell, the place of everlasting punishment. The righteous in their resurrected and glorified bodies will receive their reward and will dwell forever in Heaven with the Lord.

Isaiah 2:4; 11:9; Matthew 16:27; 18:8-9; 19:28; 24:27,30,36,44; 25:31-46; 26:64; Mark 8:38; 9:43-48; Luke 12:40,48; 16:19-26; 17:22-37; 21:27-28; John 14:1-3; Acts 1:11; 17:31; Romans 14:10; 1 Corinthians 4:5; 15:24-28,35-58; 2 Corinthians 5:10; Philippians 3:20-21; Colossians 1:5; 3:4; 1 Thessalonians 4:14-18; 5:1ff.; 2 Thessalonians 1:7ff.; 2; 1 Timothy 6:14; 2 Timothy 4:1,8; Titus 2:13; Hebrews 9:27-28; James 5:8; 2 Peter 3:7ff.; 1 John 2:28; 3:2; Jude 14; Revelation 1:18; 3:11; 20:1-22:13.

1925	1963	2000

tion in many convincing manifestations. He now exists in his glorified body at God's right hand. There will be a resurrection of the righteous and the wicked. The bodies of the righteous will conform to the glorious spiritual body of Jesus.

1 Cor. 15:1-58; 2 Cor. 5: 1-8; 1 Thess. 4:17; John 5:28-29; Phil. 3:21; Acts 24:15; John 20:9; Matt. 28:6.

XVII. The Return of the Lord

The New Testament teaches in many places the visible and personal return of Jesus to this earth. "This same Jesus which is taken up from you into heaven, shall so come in like manner as ye have seen him go into heaven." The time of his coming is not revealed. "Of that day and hour knoweth no one, no, not the angels in heaven, but my Father only" (Matt. 24:36). It is the duty of all believers to live in readiness for his coming and by diligence in good works to make manifest to all men the reality and power of their hope in Christ.

Matt. 24:36; Matt. 24:42-47; Mark 13:32-37; Luke 21:27-28; Acts 1:9-11.

Article XI: Evangelism and Missions

1925	1963	2000

It is the duty of every Christian man and woman, and the duty of every church of Christ to seek to extend the gospel to the ends of the earth. The new birth of man's spirit by God's Holy Spirit means the birth of love for others. Missionary effort on the part of all rests thus upon a spiritual necessity of the regenerate life. It is also expressly and repeatedly commanded in the teachings of Christ. It is the duty of every child of God to seek constantly to win the lost to Christ by personal effort and by all other methods sanctioned by the gospel of Christ.

It is the duty and privilege of every follower of Christ and of every church of the Lord Jesus Christ to endeavor to make disciples of all nations. The new birth of man's spirit by God's Holy Spirit means the birth of love for others. Missionary effort on the part of all rests thus upon a spiritual necessity of the regenerate life, and is expressly and repeatedly commanded in the teachings of Christ. It is the duty of every child of God to seek constantly to win the lost to Christ by personal effort and by all other methods in harmony with the gospel of Christ.

It is the duty and privilege of every follower of Christ and of every church of the Lord Jesus Christ to endeavor to make disciples of all nations. The new birth of man's spirit by God's Holy Spirit means the birth of love for others. Missionary effort on the part of all rests thus upon a spiritual necessity of the regenerate life, and is expressly and repeatedly commanded in the teachings of Christ. The Lord Jesus Christ has commanded the preaching of the gospel to all nations. It is the duty of every child of God to seek constantly to win the lost to Christ by verbal witness undergirded by a Christian lifestyle, and by other methods in harmony with the gospel of Christ.

Matt. 10:5; 13:18-23; 22:9-10; 28:19-20; Mark 16:15-16; 16:19-20; Luke 24:46-53; Acts 1:5-8; 2:1-2,21,39; 8:26-40; 10:42-48; 13:2,30-33; 1 Thess. 1:8.

Note: Article XXIII was titled "Evangelism and Missions" in the 1925 BF&M.

Gen. 12:1-3; Ex. 19:5-6; Isa. 6:1-8; Matt. 9:37-38; 10:5-15; 13:18-30,37-43; 16:19; 22:9-10; 24:14; 28:18-20; Luke 10:1-18; 24:46-53; John 14:11-12; 15:7-8,16; 17:15; 20:21; Acts 1:8; 2; 8:26-40; 10:42-48; 13:2-3; Rom. 10:13-15; Ephes. 3:1-11; 1 Thess. 1:8; 2 Tim. 4:5;

Genesis 12:1-3; Exodus 19:5-6; Isaiah 6:1-8; Matthew 9:37-38; 10:5-15; 13:18-30, 37-43; 16:19; 22:9-10; 24:14; 28:18-20; Luke 10:1-18; 24:46-53; John 14:11-12; 15:7-8,16; 17:15; 20:21; Acts 1:8; 2; 8:26-40; 10:42-48; 13:2-3; Romans 10:13-

1925	1963	2000
	Heb. 2:1-3; 11:39-12:2; 1 *Peter* 2:4-10; *Rev.* 22:17.	15; *Ephesians* 3:1-11; 1 *Thessalonians* 1:8; 2 *Timothy* 4:5; *Hebrews* 2:1-3; 11:39-12:2; 1 *Peter* 2:4-10; *Revelation* 22:17.

Article XII: Education

1925	1963	2000

Christianity is the religion of enlightenment and intelligence. In Jesus Christ are hidden all the treasures of wisdom and knowledge. All sound learning is therefore a part of our Christian heritage. The new birth opens all human faculties and creates a thirst for knowledge. An adequate system of schools is necessary to a complete spiritual program for Christ's people. The cause of education in the Kingdom of Christ is coordinate with the causes of missions and general benevolence, and should receive along with these the liberal support of the churches.

The cause of education in the kingdom of Christ is co-ordinate with the causes of missions and general benevolence and should receive along with these the liberal support of the churches. An adequate system of Christian schools is necessary to a complete spiritual program for Christ's people.

In Christian education there should be a proper balance between academic freedom and academic responsibility. Freedom in any orderly relationship of human life is always limited and never absolute. The freedom of a teacher in a Christian school, college, or seminary is limited by the pre-eminence of Jesus Christ, by the authoritative nature of the Scriptures, and by the distinct purpose for which the school exists.

Christianity is the faith of enlightenment and intelligence. In Jesus Christ abide all the treasures of wisdom and knowledge. All sound learning is, therefore, a part of our Christian heritage. The new birth opens all human faculties and creates a thirst for knowledge. Moreover, the cause of education in the Kingdom of Christ is co-ordinate with the causes of missions and general benevolence, and should receive along with these the liberal support of the churches. An adequate system of Christian education is necessary to a complete spiritual program for Christ's people.

In Christian education there should be a proper balance between academic freedom and academic responsibility. Freedom in any orderly relationship of human life is always limited and never absolute. The freedom of a teacher in a Christian school, college, or seminary is limited by the pre-eminence of Jesus Christ, by the authoritative nature of

1925	1963	2000

the Scriptures, and by the distinct purpose for which the school exists.

Deut. 4:1,5,9,13-14; Deut. 6:1,7-10; Psalm 19:7-8; Prov. 8:1-7; Prov. 4:1-10; Matt. 28:20; Col. 2:3; Neh. 8:1-4.

Note: Article XX was titled "Education" in the 1925 BF&M.

Deut. 4:1,5,9,14; 6:1-10; 31:12-13; Neh. 8:1-8; Job 28:28; Psalms 19:7ff.; 119:11; Prov. 3:13ff.; 4:1-10; 8:1-7,11; 15:14; Eccl. 7:19; Matt. 5:2; 7:24ff.; 28:19-20; Luke 2:40; 1 Cor. 1:18-31; Eph. 4:11-16; Phil. 4:8; Col. 2:3,8-9; 1 Tim. 1:3-7; 2 Tim. 2:15; 3:14-17; Heb. 5:12-6:3; James 1:5; 3:17.

Deuteronomy 4:1,5,9,14; 6:1-10; 31:12-13; Nehemiah 8:1-8; Job 28:28; Psalms 19:7ff.; 119:11; Proverbs 3:13ff.; 4:1-10; 8:1-7,11; 15:14; Ecclesiastes 7:19; Matthew 5:2; 7:24ff.; 28:19-20; Luke 2:40; 1 Corinthians 1:18-31; Ephesians 4:11-16; Philippians 4:8; Colossians 2:3,8-9; 1 Timothy 1:3-7; 2 Timothy 2:15; 3:14-17; Hebrews 5:12-6:3; James 1:5; 3:17.

Article XIII: Stewardship

1925	1963	2000

God is the source of all blessings, temporal and spiritual; all that we have and are we owe to him. We have a spiritual debtorship to the whole world, a holy trusteeship in the gospel, and a binding stewardship in our possessions. We are therefore under obligation to serve him with our time, talents and material possessions; and should recognize all these as entrusted to us to use for the glory of God and helping others. Christians should cheerfully, regularly, systematically, proportionately, and liberally, contribute of their means to advancing the Redeemer's cause on earth.

God is the source of all blessings, temporal and spiritual; all that we have and are we owe to Him. Christians have a spiritual debtorship to the whole world, a holy trusteeship in the gospel, and a binding stewardship in their possessions. They are therefore under obligation to serve Him with their time, talents, and material possessions; and should recognize all these as entrusted to them to use for the glory of God and for helping others. According to the Scriptures, Christians should contribute of their means cheerfully, regularly, systematically, proportionately, and liberally for the advancement of the Redeemer's cause on earth.

God is the source of all blessings, temporal and spiritual; all that we have and are we owe to Him. Christians have a spiritual debtorship to the whole world, a holy trusteeship in the gospel, and a binding stewardship in their possessions. They are therefore under obligation to serve Him with their time, talents, and material possessions; and should recognize all these as entrusted to them to use for the glory of God and for helping others. According to the Scriptures, Christians should contribute of their means cheerfully, regularly, systematically, proportionately, and liberally for the advancement of the Redeemer's cause on earth.

Luke 12:42; 16:1-8; Titus 1:7; 1 Peter 4:10; 2 Cor. 8:1-7; 2 Cor. 8:11-19; 2 Cor. 12:1-15; Matt. 25:14-30; Rom. 1:8-15; 1 Cor. 6:20; Acts 2:44-47.

Note: Article XXIV was titled "Stewardship" in the 1925 BF&M.

Gen. 14:20; Lev. 27:30-32; Deut. 8:18; Mal. 3:8-12; Matt. 6:1-4,19-21; 19:21; 23:23; 25:14-29; Luke 12:16-21,42; 16:1-13; Acts 2:44-47; 5:1-11; 17:24-25; 20:35; Rom. 6:6-22; 12:1-2; 1 Cor. 4:1-2; 6:19-20; 12; 16:1-4; 2 Cor. 8-9; 12:15; Phil. 4:10-19; 1 Peter 1:18-19.

Genesis 14:20; Leviticus 27:30-32; Deuteronomy 8:18; Malachi 3:8-12; Matthew 6:1-4,19-21; 19:21; 23:23; 25:14-29; Luke 12:16-21,42; 16:1-13; Acts 2:44-47; 5:1-11; 17:24-25; 20:35; Romans 6:6-22; 12:1-2; 1 Corinthians 4:1-2; 6:19-20; 12; 16:1-4; 2 Corinthians 8-9; 12:15; Philippians 4:10-19; 1 Peter 1:18-19.

Article XIV: Cooperation

1925	1963	2000

Christ's people should, as occasion requires, organize such associations and conventions as may best secure co-operation for the great objects of the Kingdom of God. Such organizations have no authority over each other or over the churches. They are voluntary and advisory bodies designed to elicit, combine and direct the energies of our people in the most effective manner. Individual members of New Testament churches should co-operate with each other, and the churches themselves should co-operate with each other in carrying forward the missionary, educational and benevolent program for the extension of Christ's Kingdom. Christian unity in the New Testament sense is spiritual harmony and voluntary co-operation for common ends by various groups of Christ's people. It is permissible and desirable as between the various Christian denominations, when the end to be attained is itself justified, and when such co-operation involves no violation of conscience or compro-

Christ's people should, as occasion requires, organize such associations and conventions as may best secure co-operation for the great objects of the kingdom of God. Such organizations have no authority over one another or over the churches. They are voluntary and advisory bodies designed to elicit, combine, and direct the energies of our people in the most effective manner. Members of New Testament churches should co-operate with one another in carrying forward the missionary, educational, and benevolent ministries for the extension of Christ's kingdom. Christian unity in the New Testament sense is spiritual harmony and voluntary co-operation for common ends by various groups of Christ's people. Co-operation is desirable between the various Christian denominations, when the end to be attained is itself justified, and when such co-operation involves no violation of conscience or compromise of loyalty to Christ and his Word as revealed in the New Testament.

Christ's people should, as occasion requires, organize such associations and conventions as may best secure cooperation for the great objects of the Kingdom of God. Such organizations have no authority over one another or over the churches. They are voluntary and advisory bodies designed to elicit, combine, and direct the energies of our people in the most effective manner. Members of New Testament churches should cooperate with one another in carrying forward the missionary, educational, and benevolent ministries for the extension of Christ's Kingdom. Christian unity in the New Testament sense is spiritual harmony and voluntary cooperation for common ends by various groups of Christ's people. Cooperation is desirable between the various Christian denominations, when the end to be attained is itself justified, and when such cooperation involves no violation of conscience or compromise of loyalty to Christ and His Word as revealed in the New Testament.

1925	1963	2000

mise of loyalty to Christ
and his Word as revealed
in the New Testament.

*Ezra 1:3-4; 2:68-69;
5:14-15; Neh. 4:4-6;
8:1-4; Mal. 3:10; Matt.
10:5-15; 20:1-16;
22:1-10; Acts 1:13-14;
1:21-26; 2:1,41-47; 1
Cor. 1:10-17; 12:11-12;
13; 14:33-34,40; 16:2; 2
Cor. 9:1-15; Eph. 4:1-16;
3 John 5-8.*

Note: *Article XXII was
titled "Co-Operation" in
the 1925 BF&M.*

*Ex. 17:12; 18:17ff.;
Judg. 7:21; Ezra 1:3-4;
2:68-69; 5:14-15; Neh.
4; 8:1-5; Matt. 10:5-15;
20:1-16; 22:1-10; 28:19-
20; Mark 2:3; Luke
10:1ff.; Acts 1:13-14;
2:1ff.; 4:31-37; 13:2-3;
15:1-35; 1 Cor. 1:10-17;
3:5-15; 12; 2 Cor. 8-9;
Gal. 1:6-10; Eph. 4:1-16;
Phil. 1:15-18.*

Note: *Article XIV was
titled "Co-Operation" in
the 1963 BF&M.*

*Exodus 17:12; 18:17ff.;
Judges 7:21; Ezra 1:3-
4; 2:68-69; 5:14-15;
Nehemiah 4; 8:1-5;
Matthew 10:5-15; 20:1-
16; 22:1-10; 28:19-20;
Mark 2:3; Luke 10:1ff.;
Acts 1:13-14; 2:1ff.;
4:31-37; 13:2-3; 15:1-35;
1 Corinthians 1:10-17;
3:5-15; 12; 2 Corinthians
8-9; Galatians 1:6-10;
Ephesians 4:1-16; Philip-
pians 1:15-18.*

Article XV: The Christian and the Social Order

1925	1963	2000

Every Christian is under obligation to seek to make the will of Christ regnant in his own life and in human society to oppose in the spirit of Christ every form of greed, selfishness, and vice; to provide for the orphaned, the aged, the helpless, and the sick; to seek to bring industry, government, and society as a whole under the sway of the principles of righteousness, truth and brotherly love; to promote these ends Christians should be ready to work with all men of good will in any good cause, always being careful to act in the spirit of love without compromising their loyalty to Christ and his truth. All means and methods used in social service for the amelioration of society and the establishment of righteousness among men must finally depend on the regeneration of the individual by the saving grace of God in Christ Jesus.

Every Christian is under obligation to seek to make the will of Christ supreme in his own life and in human society. Means and methods used for the improvement of society and the establishment of righteousness among men can be truly and permanently helpful only when they are rooted in the regeneration of the individual by the saving grace of God in Christ Jesus. The Christian should oppose in the spirit of Christ every form of greed, selfishness, and vice. He should work to provide for the orphaned, the needy, the aged, the helpless, and the sick. Every Christian should seek to bring industry, government, and society as a whole under the sway of the principles of righteousness, truth, and brotherly love. In order to promote these ends Christians should be ready to work with all men of good will in any good cause, always being careful to act in the spirit of love without compromising their loyalty to Christ and his truth.

All Christians are under obligation to seek to make the will of Christ supreme in our own lives and in human society. Means and methods used for the improvement of society and the establishment of righteousness among men can be truly and permanently helpful only when they are rooted in the regeneration of the individual by the saving grace of God in Jesus Christ. In the spirit of Christ, Christians should oppose racism, every form of greed, selfishness, and vice, and all forms of sexual immorality, including adultery, homosexuality, and pornography. We should work to provide for the orphaned, the needy, the abused, the aged, the helpless, and the sick. We should speak on behalf of the unborn and contend for the sanctity of all human life from conception to natural death. Every Christian should seek to bring industry, government, and society as a whole under the sway of the principles of righteousness, truth, and brotherly love. In order to promote these ends Christians should be ready to work

1925	1963	2000
		with all men of good will in any good cause, always being careful to act in the spirit of love without compromising their loyalty to Christ and His truth.

1925	1963	2000
Luke 10:25-37; Ex. 22:10,14; Lev. 6:2; Deut. 20:10; Deut. 4:42; Deut. 15:2; 27:17; Psalm 101:5; Ezek. 18:6; Heb. 2:15; Zech. 8:16; Ex. 20:16; James 2:8; Rom. 12-14; Col. 3:12-17.	*Ex. 20:3-17; Lev. 6:2-5; Deut. 10:12; 27:17; Psalm 101:5; Micah 6:8; Zech. 8:16; Matt. 5:13-16,43-48; 22:36-40; 25:35; Mark 1:29-34; 2:3ff.; 10:21; Luke 4:18-21; 10:27-37; 20:25; John 15:12; 17:15; Rom. 12-14; 1 Cor. 5:9-10; 6:1-7; 7:20-24; 10:23-11:1; Gal. 3:26-28; Eph. 6:5-9; Col. 3:12-17; 1 Thess. 3:12; Philemon; James 1:27; 2:8.*	*Exodus 20:3-17; Leviticus 6:2-5; Deuteronomy 10:12; 27:17; Psalm 101:5; Micah 6:8; Zechariah 8:16; Matthew 5:13-16,43-48; 22:36-40; 25:35; Mark 1:29-34; 2:3ff.; 10:21; Luke 4:18-21; 10:27-37; 20:25; John 15:12; 17:15; Romans 12-14; 1 Corinthians 5:9-10; 6:1-7; 7:20-24; 10:23-11:1; Galatians 3:26-28; Ephesians 6:5-9; Colossians 3:12-17; 1 Thessalonians 3:12; Philemon; James 1:27; 2:8.*
Note: Article XXI was titled "Social Service" in the 1925 BF&M.		

Article XVI: Peace and War

1925	1963	2000

It is the duty of Christians to seek peace with all men on principles of righteousness. In accordance with the spirit and teachings of Christ they should do all in their power to put an end to war.

The true remedy for the war spirit is the pure gospel of our Lord. The supreme need of the world is the acceptance of his teachings in all the affairs of men and nations, and the practical application of his law of love.

We urge Christian people throughout the world to pray for the reign of the Prince of Peace, and to oppose everything likely to provoke war.

Matt. 5:9,13-14,43-46; Heb. 12:14; James 4:1; Matt. 6:33; Rom. 14:17,19.

Note: Article XIX was titled "Peace and War" in the 1925 BF&M.

It is the duty of Christians to seek peace with all men on principles of righteousness. In accordance with the spirit and teachings of Christ they should do all in their power to put an end to war.

The true remedy for the war spirit is the gospel of our Lord. The supreme need of the world is the acceptance of His teachings in all the affairs of men and nations, and the practical application of His law of love.

Isa. 2:4; Matt. 5:9,38-48; 6:33; 26:52; Luke 22:36,38; Rom. 12:18-19; 13:1-7; 14:19; Heb.12:14; James 4:1-2.

It is the duty of Christians to seek peace with all men on principles of righteousness. In accordance with the spirit and teachings of Christ they should do all in their power to put an end to war.

The true remedy for the war spirit is the gospel of our Lord. The supreme need of the world is the acceptance of His teachings in all the affairs of men and nations, and the practical application of His law of love. Christian people throughout the world should pray for the reign of the Prince of Peace.

Isaiah 2:4; Matthew 5:9,38-48; 6:33; 26:52; Luke 22:36,38; Romans 12:18-19; 13:1-7; 14:19; Hebrews 12:14; James 4:1-2.

Article XVII: Religious Liberty

1925	1963	2000

God alone is Lord of the conscience, and he has left it free from the doctrines and commandments of men which are contrary to his Word or not contained in it. Church and state should be separate. The state owes to the church protection and full freedom in the pursuit of its spiritual ends. In providing for such freedom no ecclesiastical group or denomination should be favored by the state more than others. Civil government being ordained of God, it is the duty of Christians to render loyal obedience thereto in all things not contrary to the revealed will of God. The church should not resort to the civil power to carry on its work. The gospel of Christ contemplates spiritual means alone for the pursuit of its ends. The state has no right to impose penalties for religious opinions of any kind. The state has no right to impose taxes for the support of any form of religion. A free church in a free state is the Christian ideal, and this implies the right of free and unhindered access to God on the part

God alone is Lord of the conscience, and He has left it free from the doctrines and commandments of men which are contrary to His Word or not contained in it. Church and state should be separate. The state owes to every church protection and full freedom in the pursuit of its spiritual ends. In providing for such freedom no ecclesiastical group or denomination should be favored by the state more than others. Civil government being ordained of God, it is the duty of Christians to render loyal obedience thereto in all things not contrary to the revealed will of God. The church should not resort to the civil power to carry on its work. The gospel of Christ contemplates spiritual means alone for the pursuit of its ends. The state has no right to impose penalties for religious opinions of any kind. The state has no right to impose taxes for the support of any form of religion. A free church in a free state is the Christian ideal, and this implies the right of free and unhindered access to God on the part

God alone is Lord of the conscience, and He has left it free from the doctrines and commandments of men which are contrary to His Word or not contained in it. Church and state should be separate. The state owes to every church protection and full freedom in the pursuit of its spiritual ends. In providing for such freedom no ecclesiastical group or denomination should be favored by the state more than others. Civil government being ordained of God, it is the duty of Christians to render loyal obedience thereto in all things not contrary to the revealed will of God. The church should not resort to the civil power to carry on its work. The gospel of Christ contemplates spiritual means alone for the pursuit of its ends. The state has no right to impose penalties for religious opinions of any kind. The state has no right to impose taxes for the support of any form of religion. A free church in a free state is the Christian ideal, and this implies the right of free and unhindered access to God on the part

1925	1963	2000

of all men, and the right to form and propagate opinions in the sphere of religion without interference by the civil power.

Rom. 13:1-7; 1 Peter 2:17; 1 Tim. 2:1-2; Gal. 3:9-14; John 7:38-39; James 4:12; Gal. 5:13; 2 Peter 2:18-21; 1 Cor. 3:5; Rom. 6:1-2; Matt. 22:21; Mark 12:17.

Note: Article XVIII was titled "Religious Liberty" in the 1925 BF&M.

of all men and the right to form and propagate opinions in the sphere of religion without interference by the civil power.

Gen. 1:27; 2:7; Matt. 6:6-7,24; Matt 16:26; Matt 22:21; John 8:36; Acts 4:19-20; Rom. 6:1-2; 13:1-7; Gal. 5:1,13; Phil. 3:20; 1 Tim. 2:1-2; James 4:12; 1 Peter 2:12-17; 3:11-17; 4:12-19

of all men, and the right to form and propagate opinions in the sphere of religion without interference by the civil power.

Genesis 1:27; 2:7; Matthew 6:6-7, 24; 16:26; 22:21; John 8:36; Acts 4:19-20; Romans 6:1-2; 13:1-7; Galatians 5:1,13; Philippians 3:20; 1 Timothy 2:1-2; James 4:12; 1 Peter 2:12-17; 3:11-17; 4:12-19.

Article XVIII: The Family

1925	1963	2000

Note: The 1925 BF&M did not specifically address this topic.

God has ordained the family as the foundational institution of human society. It is composed of persons related to one another by marriage, blood, or adoption.

Marriage is the uniting of one man and one woman in covenant commitment for a lifetime. It is God's unique gift to provide for the man and the woman in marriage the framework for intimate companionship, the channel for sexual expression according to biblical standards, and the means for procreation of the human race.

The husband and wife are of equal worth before God, since both are created in God's image. The marriage relationship models the way God relates to His people. A husband is to love his wife as Christ loved the church. He has the God-given responsibility to provide for, to protect, and to lead his family. A wife is to submit herself graciously to the servant leadership

God has ordained the family as the foundational institution of human society. It is composed of persons related to one another by marriage, blood, or adoption.

Marriage is the uniting of one man and one woman in covenant commitment for a lifetime. It is God's unique gift to reveal the union between Christ and His church and to provide for the man and the woman in marriage the framework for intimate companionship, the channel of sexual expression according to biblical standards, and the means for procreation of the human race.

The husband and wife are of equal worth before God, since both are created in God's image. The marriage relationship models the way God relates to His people. A husband is to love his wife as Christ loved the church. He has the God-given responsibility to provide for, to protect, and to lead his family. A wife is to submit herself graciously to the servant leadership

1925	1963	2000
	of her husband even as the church willingly submits to the headship of Christ. She, being in the image of God as is her husband and thus equal to him, has the God-given responsibility to respect her husband and to serve as his helper in managing the household and nurturing the next generation.	of her husband even as the church willingly submits to the headship of Christ. She, being in the image of God as is her husband and thus equal to him, has the God-given responsibility to respect her husband and to serve as his helper in managing the household and nurturing the next generation.
	Children, from the moment of conception, are a blessing and heritage from the Lord. Parents are to demonstrate to their children God's pattern for marriage. Parents are to teach their children spiritual and moral values and to lead them, through consistent lifestyle example and loving discipline, to make choices based on biblical truth. Children are to honor and obey their parents.	Children, from the moment of conception, are a blessing and heritage from the Lord. Parents are to demonstrate to their children God's pattern for marriage. Parents are to teach their children spiritual and moral values and to lead them, through consistent lifestyle example and loving discipline, to make choices based on biblical truth. Children are to honor and obey their parents.
	Gen. 1:26-28; 2:18-25; 3:1-20; Ex. 20:12; Deut. 6:4-9; Josh. 24:15; 1 Sam. 1:26-28; Ps. 51:5; 78:1-8; 127; 128; 139:13-16; Prov. 1:8; 5:15-20; 6:20-22; 12:4; 13:24; 14:1; 17:6; 18:22; 22:6,15; 23:13-14; 24:3; 29:15,17; 31:10-31; Eccl. 4:9-12; 9:9; Mal. 2:14-16; Matt. 5:31-32; 18:2-5; 19:3-9; Mark	*Genesis 1:26-28; 2:15-25; 3:1-20; Exodus 20:12; Deuteronomy 6:4-9; Joshua 24:15; 1 Samuel 1:26-28; Psalms 51:5; 78:1-8; 127; 128; 139:13-16; Proverbs 1:8; 5:15-20; 6:20-22; 12:4; 13:24; 14:1; 17:6; 18:22; 22:6,15; 23:13-14; 24:3; 29:15,17; 31:10-31; Ecclesiastes 4:9-12; 9:9; Malachi 2:14-16;*

1925	1963	2000
	10:6-12; Rom. 1:18-32; 1 Cor. 7:1-16; Eph. 5:21-33; 6:1-4; Col. 3:18-21; 1 Tim. 5:8,14; 2 Tim. 1:3-5; Titus 2:3-5; Heb. 13:4; 1 Pet. 3:1-7. *Note: This article was added to the 1963 BF&M through an amendment in 1998.*	Matthew 5:31-32; 18:2-5; 19:3-9; Mark 10:6-12; Romans 1:18-32; 1 Corinthians 7:1-16; Ephesians 5:21-33; 6:1-4; Colossians 3:18-21; 1 Timothy 5:8,14; 2 Timothy 1:3-5; Titus 2:3-5; Hebrews 13:4; 1 Peter 3:1-7.

Appendix II
Missouri Baptists and the Cooperative Program

What is the Cooperative Program?

The Cooperative Program (CP) is the funding process Southern Baptists have used since 1925 to support missions at the state, national, and international levels. Through CP, the ministry reach of your church extends around the world as 47,000 cooperating Southern Baptist churches join hands to fulfill the Great Commission.

How does CP work?

The Cooperative Program begins with you and your tithes and offerings to your Missouri Baptist church. Your church, in turn, shares a portion of its annual budget with the Cooperative Program, sending its CP gifts to the Missouri Baptist Convention (MBC), which distributes CP funds from 1,800 MBC-affiliated churches according to an approved plan.

Specifically, 35 cents of each CP dollar support Missouri Baptist causes such as evangelism, church planting, disaster relief, and collegiate ministries. Another 22 cents help fund the ministries of MBC institutions: the Missouri Baptist Children's Home, Baptist Homes & Healthcare Ministries, three universities, and the Missouri Baptist Foundation. Five cents provide Missouri pastor benefits through

GuideStone, along with production and distribution of *The Pathway*, the MBC's news journal.

Finally, 38 cents go to the Southern Baptist Convention to support nearly 9,000 full-time missionaries, six seminaries, and ethics and religious liberty.

Why give through the Cooperative Program?

Your CP giving comes back to you – in training, events, resources, consultation, church-staff retirement and insurance benefits, and other ministries for the local church.

CP supports evangelism, discipleship, church planting and revitalization, disaster relief, foster care, rescue from human trafficking, ministries to the aged, Christian higher education, student and collegiate ministries, hunger relief, partnership missions, transitional pastor training, Missouri Baptist news and information, and much more – and that's just in Missouri.

The Cooperative Program enables every giver and every local church to make an impact for Christ in Missouri, throughout North America, and around the world.

How the Cooperative Program Works

When you give to your church, a portion goes to the Cooperative Program (CP), which advances the gospel in Missouri, across North America, and around the world.

Here's how CP works, in three easy steps:

1 You give to your local Missouri Baptist church.

2 Your church shares a portion through the Cooperative Program.

3 The combined CP giving of nearly 1,800 Missouri Baptist churches supports ministries across our state, throughout North America, and around the world.

CP enables every giver and every local church to make an impact for Christ.

Learn more about the Cooperative Program at mobaptist.org/cp.

 COOPERATIVE PROGRAM

 MISSOURI BAPTISTS

How Your Cooperative Program Dollar Is Invested

When your church gives through the Cooperative Program, here's how each $1 helps transform lives and communities with the gospel.*

Missouri Baptist Causes

$0.02	Making Disciples
$0.05	Multiplying Churches
$0.04	Developing Leaders
$0.06	Collegiate Ministries
$0.11	Executive Office
$0.07	Ministry Support & Apologetics

Missouri Baptist Entities

$0.04	Missouri Baptist Children's Home
$0.16	Christian Higher Education
$0.01	Baptist Homes & Healthcare Ministries
$0.01	Missouri Baptist Foundation

Southern Baptist Causes

$0.19	International Mission Board
$0.09	North American Mission Board
$0.08	Theological Education
$0.01	Ethics & Religious Liberty Commission
$0.01	Executive Committee

SBC/MBC Shared Administration

$0.05	GuideStone Pastor Protection; The Pathway

$1.00

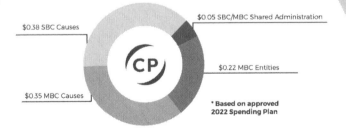

$0.38 SBC Causes

$0.35 MBC Causes

$0.05 SBC/MBC Shared Administration

$0.22 MBC Entities

*Based on approved 2022 Spending Plan

Answers to Questions for Personal or Group Study

Article I: The Scriptures

1. The Bible is the written word of God. He is the author of Scripture, revealing truths we are incapable of knowing without divine help. Because God is the source of Scripture, we may say the Bible is a perfect treasure of divine instruction.

2. *General revelation* is how God reveals himself to all people in creation and conscience; it leaves us without an excuse for rejecting him (Rom. 1:18-32). *Special revelation* is a record of God's work before time, in time, and beyond time, with a particular emphasis on creation, sin, redemption, and restoration. The Bible and Jesus are two specific forms of special revelation.

3. The Bible is inspired, inerrant, infallible, and sufficient.

4. The correct answer is (c).

5. True, True, False, True, False.

Article II: God

1. The *Shema* is an affirmation of Judaism and a declaration of faith in one God. It's important to our understanding of God because it shows how the one living and true God reveals himself to humans from ancient times, and it sets the stage for all that God's word teaches about the triune God throughout the Old and New Testaments.

2. Demons.

3. The correct answer is (b).

4. We believe in the Trinity because God reveals himself in Scripture as one living and true God in three persons. As we read God's progressive revelation – from Genesis through the Book of Revelation – this doctrine becomes clear.

5. See the correct answers below:

	Order
Matthew 28:19-20	Father, Son, Spirit
Romans 8:1-3	Son, Spirit, Father
2 Corinthians 13:14 (13:13 in CSB)	Son, Father, Spirit
Galatians 4:6	Father, Spirit, Son
1 John 4:2	Spirit, Son, Father
Jude 20	Spirit, Father, Son

Article II-A: God the Father

1. Scripture describes God as spirit, not flesh and blood as human beings are. At the same time, the Father is a person who relates to other members of the Godhead, as well as to human beings made in his image.

2. God the Father.

3. False, False, True, True, True.

4. The Father and Jesus have eternally existed in an intimate relationship with one another. For Jesus to refer to God as his father illustrates the distinction between the persons of the Godhead but does

not imply rank or levels of superiority. The Father, Son, and Holy Spirit are co-equal and co-eternal.

5. Matthew 5:48 - perfect; Matthew 6:32 – all-knowing; John 17:3 – true deity; Romans 1:20 – eternal power; 1 Timothy 1:17 – immortal; Revelation 19:6 - almighty.

Article II-B: God the Son

1. The doctrine of the Incarnation means the eternal Son of God took on human flesh in the person of Jesus of Nazareth. As such, Jesus is one person in two natures: divine and human.

2. Matthew 28:18 – claims omnipotence; Mark 2:1-12 – forgives sins; John 8:13-20 – teaches with divine authority; John 8:58 – uses divine expression *I AM*; John 10:30 – claims equality with the Father; John 20:28 – receives worship.

3. Jesus chooses, in certain instances, not to avail himself of certain divine attributes so that he might fully identify with sinful and fallen human beings.

4. Here are four observations: (a) Jesus exists in very nature as God, with the inner divine substance that is God's alone; (b) in the Incarnation, Jesus fulfills his mission as the servant of all; (c) as Jesus becomes human, he loses nothing of his divine nature; (d) to obey the Father to the point of death requires the ability to die, and for this, Jesus has to be human.

5. The correct answer is (d).

Article II-C: God the Holy Spirit

1. The Jehovah's Witness view of the Holy Spirit denies his personhood and deity. The Muslim view also denies the deity of the Spirit and makes him a lesser, created being. The proper biblical view is that the

Holy Spirit is the third person of the Trinity, co-equal and co-eternal with the Father and the Son.

2. We probably don't intentionally minimize the person and work of the Holy Spirit, but sometimes we focus our attention on our Heavenly Father, who adopts us as his children, and on Jesus as our Savior, without thinking about the important work of the Spirit in creation, redemption, and the revelation of Scripture. We should remember that the Spirit is co-equal and co-eternal with the other members of the Godhead.

3. True, True, False, True, False.

4. Genesis 1:1-2 – creates; Matthew 28:19 – shares a divine name with the Father and the Son; John 16:7-11 – convicts unbelievers; Acts 13:1-2 – calls to Christian service; Romans 8:26-27 – intercedes in prayer; 1 Corinthians 12:6, 11 – distributes spiritual gifts.

5. Acts 5:1-11 reveals that the Holy Spirit is a person. He also is divine. He may be lied to and sinned against. The consequences of sinning against the Holy Spirit may be severe, including physical death (cf. 1 Cor. 11:27-32).

Article III: Man

1. The phrase *imago dei* refers to the image of God, in which all people are created. By making all human beings in his image, God sets humanity apart from the rest of creation. Every person, regardless of ethnicity, gender, age, abilities, socioeconomic class, or even behavior, retains God-given worth and dignity.

2. The BF&M 2000 addresses shifting attitudes toward gender, which many in society now view as "fluid," or a matter of personal choice rather than a gift from God. Christians should stand on the unchanging truth of Scripture, while dealing compassionately with those who struggle with gender confusion.

3. The correct answer is (c).

4. Consequences of the Fall (Gen. 3) include: shame; alienation from God; death of the body, soul, and spirit; human conflict, even within marriage; difficulty in childbirth; the struggle to eke a living out of a cursed environment; and banishment from Eden. The Fall also affects Satan, who is cursed. There is good news for mankind, however: the Lord promises to send a redeemer who will crush the serpent's head; this is fulfilled in the virgin-born Messiah, Jesus of Nazareth.

5. In 2 Peter 3:10-13, Peter tells us Jesus is coming back to purge the world of sin and its stain. In the process, he is creating new heavens and a new earth in which righteousness dwells. In Revelation 21:4, John sees a day when God wipes every tear from our eyes. Death, grief, crying, and pain are no more.

Article IV: Salvation

1. Salvation is God's remedy for the sin that has ruined everything and alienated everyone from him. Salvation is God's gift of forgiveness and everlasting life, granted through the death, burial, and resurrection of Christ. It is received by faith.

2. See the correct answers below:

	Who?	From what?
Deuteronomy 20:4	Israelites	Their enemies
Daniel 6:20	Daniel	Lions
Psalm 7:10	The righteous	The wicked
Acts 27:22, 31, 34	Paul	Shipwreck
Philippians 1:19	Paul	Danger; false accusations

3. See the correct answers below:

	Past, present, or future?
Sanctification	Present
Election	Past
Glorification	Future
Justification	Present
Foreknowledge	Past
Regeneration	Present
Indwelling	Present
Spirit baptism	Present
Predestination	Past
Adoption	Present
Sealing	Present
Calling	Present

4. The correct answer is (d).

5. We *were saved* from the penalty of sin. We *are being saved* from the power of sin. And we *will be saved* from the presence of sin.

Article IV-A: Regeneration

1. The Holy Spirit is the agent of regeneration, which also is known as being born again, born from above, and born of the Spirit.

2. Matthew 19:28 applies to the future work of Christ, when he creates new heavens and a new earth. Titus 3:5 refers to the work of the Holy Spirit, making a sinner spiritually alive.

3. John 3:18 – condemned in their unbelief; 2 Corinthians 4:4 – blinded in their minds; Ephesians 2:1 – dead in trespasses and sins; Colossians 1:21 – enemies of the Lord; 2 Timothy 2:26 – bound by Satan; 1 Peter 2:9 – in spiritual darkness.

4. *Baptismal regeneration* is the belief that water baptism is necessary for salvation. Southern Baptists reject this doctrine as unbiblical for several reasons, including: (1) the Bible is clear that we are saved by grace alone, through faith alone, in Christ alone; (2) water baptism is an important public testimony of our faith, not an essential element in our salvation; (3) the Bible says a person is condemned for not believing, not for failing to be baptized; (4) forgiveness of sins and everlasting life are received as gifts from God, not as a result of an external act such as water baptism; (5) if water baptism is required for salvation, then no one could be saved without the help of another person.

5. A person is regenerated once by the Holy Spirit. Regeneration is a one-time, non-repeatable act and is permanent. If regeneration, or any other facet of salvation, may be lost, then all facets may be lost, and there can be no assurance of salvation.

Article IV-B: Justification

1. Justification is the act of God declaring sinners righteous on the basis of the finished work of Christ. Believers' sins are transferred to Christ's account and exchanged for his righteousness. God the Father is the author of justification.

2. False, True, True, False, True.

3. *Forensic* means "having to do with legal proceedings." Justification does not change our internal character. Judges don't make defendants guilty or not guilty; they simply declare them to be one or the other.

4. Romans 5:1 – peace with God; 2 Corinthians 5:21 – the righteousness of God imputed to the believer; Ephesians 2:8-10 – works God has prepared from eternity past; Titus 2:11-14 – new attitudes and outlooks.

5. Every person needs justification because every person is a sinner. No one possesses the righteousness necessary to enter God's presence. Our best efforts are but filthy rags in the eyes of God (Isa. 64:6).

Article IV-C: Sanctification

1. *Sanctification* is the work of God making Christians more like Jesus.

2. *Positional sanctification* is the state of being separate, set apart from the common, and dedicated to a higher purpose. It is a one-time, non-repeatable act of God in the believing sinner. *Practical sanctification* is the lifelong process by which the Spirit makes us more like Jesus. This requires our ongoing submission to Christ and our obedience to the voice of the indwelling Spirit.

3. Luke 9:23 – taking up our cross and following Jesus; Romans 8:13 – putting to death the deeds of the body; Romans 12:1-2 – presenting our

bodies as living sacrifices; Philippians 1:6 – God's promise to finish the good work he began in us; Philippians 2:13 – the Lord nurturing Christ's righteousness within us; 2 Peter 3:18 – growing in grace and in the knowledge of Jesus.

4. I do not believe it's possible to attain sinless perfection in the Christian life. Even though God has saved us from the penalty of sin, he will not save us completely from the presence and power of sin until we are glorified after our resurrection (see the next two chapters).

5. The non-perfectionist view of sanctification is more biblically faithful than the perfectionist view for three reasons: (1) sin is more subtle and pervasive than we may care to admit; (2) the Greek word translated "perfect" in Matt. 5:48 (*teleioi*) is better rendered "complete," or "mature;" (3) there is a striking absence of sinless characters in the Bible (except, of course, for Jesus).

Article IV-D: Glorification

1. In glorification, Christians are fully conformed to the image of Christ. It is the last link in God's golden chain of redemption (see Rom. 8:29-30).

2. *Glory* refers to an individual's display of splendor, wealth, and pomp (Old Testament, Heb. *kabod*), or to honor, brilliance and fame (New Testament, Gr. *doxa*). When used to describe God, it points to the greatness of his whole nature.

3. Glory now – we participate in God's moral excellence; glory in death – our souls and spirits pass into the presence of Christ in heaven; glory in resurrection – our physical bodies are raised in the likeness of Christ's glorified body; glory in restoration – Jesus creates new heavens and a new earth.

4. True, False, False, True, False.

5. Paul compares our present-day suffering with a glorious future (Rom. 8:18). We "groan within ourselves," waiting for the "redemption of our bodies" (v. 23). In a similar way, "the whole creation has been groaning together with labor pains until now" (v. 22), but creation will be "set free from the bondage to decay" (v. 21). Paul ends this passage with the so-called "golden chain of redemption," assuring us that God will finish what he started (vv. 29-30).

Article IV-D (Continued): Our Glorified Bodies

1. Christians are glorified, or fully conformed to the image of Christ, at the time of our physical resurrection. We are given incorruptible bodies similar to the body Jesus possessed when he rose from the dead.

2. Our souls / spirits are in heaven with the Lord between death and resurrection.

3. The correct answers are (b) and (d).

4. Sown in corruption ... raised in incorruption; sown in dishonor ... raised in glory; sown in weakness ... raised in power; sown a natural body ... raised a spiritual body.

5. Our physical bodies today are *natural bodies* in that they belong to the sinful and fallen world in which we live. They are subject to sickness, injury, aging, and death. Our physical bodies in glorification are similar in that they are, indeed, physical bodies. At the same time, they are *spiritual bodies* in that they belong to the Holy Spirit and to the world to come – a perfect world in which there is no more sickness, injury, aging, or death.

Article V: God's Purpose of Grace

1. Both views acknowledge the biblical doctrine of divine election, but they differ in how the doctrine is biblically defined, and how it's applied.

Unconditional election (the Reformed / Calvinist view) is the belief that God selected specific persons for everlasting life based solely on his divine will and good pleasure, not on foreseen faith. *Conditional election* (the non-Reformed / Arminian view) is the belief that God selected specific persons for salvation based on foreseeing their belief and repentance in response to the gospel message.

2. Molinism and corporate election.

3. The correct answer is (a).

4. Election is gracious and eternal ... reprobation is just and eternal; election is established in Christ ... reprobation is declared by Christ; election is conditioned on faith and repentance ... reprobation is conditioned on unbelief and rebellion; election is personal in its application ... reprobation is personal in its application.

5. The doctrine of divine election has been debated for centuries and continues to be a point of contention between Reformed / Calvinistic and non-Reformed believers, including those in Southern Baptist churches. The debate focuses on Scripture – specifically, how to understand the biblical truths of divine sovereignty and human freedom. We may find common ground in our united belief in the inerrancy of Scripture; in the certainty that Scripture teaches the doctrine of election; in the parallel biblical truths of divine sovereignty and human freedom; in the rejection of fatalism; and in the embrace of one another as brothers and sisters in Christ.

Article VI: The Church

1. The universal church is the complete body of believers who have trusted in Jesus as Lord and Savior. The local church is a body of baptized believers in Jesus who live in the same community and gather at a common place for worship, fellowship, instruction, and service.

2. See the correct answers below:

	Universal or local church?
Matthew 16:18	Universal
Acts 9:31	Local
1 Corinthians 1:2	Local
Ephesians 1:22-23	Universal
Colossians 1:18	Universal
Colossians 4:15	Local
Revelation 7:9	Universal

3. (1) As a *body*, with Christ as the head and believers as various parts of the body; (2) as a *building*, with Christ as the chief cornerstone, the teaching of the apostles as the foundation, and believers as the building stones; (3) as a *bride*, to be kept pure and eager for the coming of the bridegroom, Jesus Christ; (4) as a *mystery*, hidden from Old Testament believers but revealed to the apostles and given to Christians; and (5) as an *organization* with officers and ordinances.

4. Apostles – primarily the twelve, but also messengers sent from one church to another; prophets – public proclaimers of God's word; evangelists – those specially gifted to win souls; pastors – overseers, wise counselors, and shepherds in the local church; teachers – those specially

gifted to train others in the local church; deacons – servants in the local church, enabling pastors to focus on the word of God and prayer.

5. Five key distinctives of the local church: (1) autonomy, meaning that every local congregation has the authority to fulfill its ministry; (2) the lordship of Jesus over the church; (3) a congregation of believers who covenant together to fulfill the Great Commission; (4) a common baptism that binds us together as believers and establishes the boundaries of membership in the congregation; and (5) voluntary cooperation with other like-minded believers.

Article VII: Baptism and the Lord's Supper

1. An *ordinance* is a symbolic act of obedience that pictures the finished work of Christ and prepares believers for Christ's imminent return. A *sacrament*, as some see it, is an essential part of the salvation process. For others, a sacrament is a "means of God's grace," or a special way God speaks to our hearts and prepares us for service.

2. We are to be immersed for these reasons: (1) our identification with the crucified, buried, and risen Savior; (2) the death of our old life, and the resurrection to new life in Christ; (3) baptism by the Holy Spirit into the body of Christ, which took place at conversion; and (4) our faith in the future resurrection of the dead.

3. Two biblical truths about baptism: (1) Jesus was baptized, identifying him as the Son of God and initiating a new epoch in God's plan of redemption as the Spirit descended on him; and (2) the early Christians were gladly baptized as a testimony of their faith.

4. Exodus 12:1-28 – the Lord's Supper is tied to Passover, a remembrance of God's deliverance of the Israelites from Egyptian bondage; Luke 22:14-20 – Jesus institutes the Lord's Supper during the Passover celebration; 1 Corinthians 11:24 – the unleavened bread symbolizes the body of Jesus, which is broken for us; 1 Corinthians

11:25 – the cup symbolizes the new covenant Jesus establishes through his spilled blood on the cross; 1 Corinthians 11:26 – we proclaim the Lord's death until he returns every time we partake of the Lord's Supper; 1 Corinthians 11:27-32 – believers should carefully examine themselves before taking part in the Lord's Supper.

5. Many Southern Baptist churches require new believers, or prospective new church members, to complete a new members' class, submit to pastoral counseling, or participate in a time of testimony and examination by the church. These processes are designed to help new believers understand their salvation experience and their future responsibilities as members of a local church. As for the Lord's Supper, many Southern Baptist churches partake of the Lord's Supper on a weekly, monthly, or quarterly schedule.

Article VIII: The Lord's Day

1. False, True, False, True, False (unless you're a fan of the Las Vegas Raiders).

2. Sunday. Jesus' appearance on this day likely influenced his disciples to gather for worship on Sunday, although not necessarily at the exclusion of Saturday (the Sabbath).

3. First, Sunday observance of the Lord's Day points to the centrality of the resurrection in the Christian faith. Second, Sunday is the first day of a new creation. Third, Sunday is the "eighth day," a day related both to circumcision and also "the final day of eternal rest and joy."

4. Most Southern Baptists likely would answer no. That is, worshiping on Sunday does not violate the Fourth Commandment. One key reason for this is that Jesus fulfilled the Sabbath through his sinless life, death, burial, and resurrection, and he invites us to rest in him (Matt. 11:28-30; cf. Heb. 4:9-11).

5. We should always contend for our beliefs with gentleness and

respect (see 1 Pet. 3:15-16). Rather than engage in fruitless debates over "disputed matters" (Rom. 14), we should agree that the Bible is God's final word on the matter and thus commit to its continued study.

Article IX: The Kingdom

1. The kingdom is God's reign, his authority to rule. God is sovereign over the universe; yet a competing kingdom – the kingdom of Satan – has risen up in opposition. In the Incarnation, Jesus invaded Satan's rebel kingdom and began rescuing believing sinners out of the evil one's domain, bringing them into the kingdom of God – a mission he continues today. At the return of Christ, Satan, rebellious angels, and unrepentant people are cast out. God's kingdom comes in its fullness as Jesus restores the sinless perfection of his created world.

2. *Creation* – God creates everything and declares it "very good indeed;" *fall* – Satan rebels, Adam follows his lead, and a competing kingdom arises; *redemption* – Jesus invades Satan's kingdom and starts rescuing the evil one's captives; *restoration* – Jesus returns and creates new heavens and a new earth.

3. True, True, False, False, True.

4. Jesus casts out demons by the Spirit of God, demonstrating that the kingdom is among the people by virtue of his presence. Satan is the strong man in Jesus' parable. The religious leaders will not be forgiven because they have rejected all three persons of the Trinity, particularly the Son and the Holy Spirit. (In John 8:44, Jesus tells the religious leaders that the devil, not God, is their father, indicating they have rejected the Father as well.)

5. The *mystery* of the kingdom of God is its already / not yet quality. That means the kingdom must first come without fanfare in the Lamb of God who takes away the sin of the world. The kingdom is present where Jesus is present – on the earth briefly two thousand years ago, and today

in the hearts of believers. When Jesus returns, the kingdom comes in its fullness.

Article X: Last Things

1. Future events tend to captivate people's attention. Modern media, with its imaginative story-telling and dazzling technical capabilities, seize our fascination with the future. Further, virtually all belief systems, including atheism, foretell an end of the world. For Christians, the Bible makes it clear Christ is returning, and the world as we know it is ending.

2. I'd love to hear about your favorite apocalyptic book, movie, or television series. Send me a brief note at rphillips@mobaptist.org.

3. Matthew 24:36 – the world ends when the Father says so; John 5:28-29 – the world ends with the resurrection of the dead; 2 Peter 3:10-13 – the world ends with the creation of new heavens and a new earth; Revelation 21:3 – the world ends as it began, with God dwelling with us; Revelation 22:12 – the world ends with judgment.

4. False, False, True, True, False.

5. Death, grief, crying, and pain; these are described as "former things" (Rev. 21:4).

Article XI: Evangelism and Missions

1. Evangelism is sharing the gospel with the goal of leading others to repentance and faith in Jesus. Missions may be defined as the church's responsibility to bring God's love and the Christian gospel to all people through evangelism, education, and ministry. Evangelism and missions are related to each other in that evangelism is a primary means by which Christians bring God's love and the gospel to all people.

2. An angel is a messenger, or one who is sent. Christians are messengers sent to proclaim the gospel.

3. There are many counterfeit gospels (2 Cor. 11:4). Some false gospels deny that Jesus is the way, the truth, and the life (John 14:6). Others add works to faith as necessary for salvation. And others are universalist, declaring that all paths ultimately lead to God. But there is only one true gospel: the gospel of salvation by grace alone, through faith alone, in Christ alone.

4. True, False, True, False, True, False.

5. Jesus says the Holy Spirit convicts (or convinces) unbelievers of sin, righteousness, and judgment. By *sin*, he means the hardened unbelief that keeps sinners from trusting in their only provision for sin: Jesus. By *righteousness*, he means the necessary righteousness of Christ, who is our only hope of justification. And by *judgment*, he means the damnation of Satan, which unrepentant sinners ultimately share.

Article XII: Education

1. Education must be grounded in what God has revealed to us. We are to embrace truth, teach it to our children, model it in our lives, proclaim it in our churches, and share it with the world.

2. Psalm 19:1 – God reveals himself in creation; John 14:9 – God reveals himself in the person of Christ; Romans 2:15-16 – God reveals himself in conscience; 2 Timothy 3:16-17 – God reveals himself in the canon of Scripture.

3. We are to take advantage of every opportunity to teach God's words "when you sit in your house and when you walk along the road, when you lie down and when you get up. Bind them as a sign on your hand and let them be a symbol on your forehead. Write them on the doorposts of your house and on your city gates" (Deut. 6:7-9).

4. Local churches organize comprehensive teaching and training ministries for their members. At the same time, Southern Baptists cooperate at the associational, state, and national levels to support Christian education. Depending on how members of 47,000 autonomous Southern Baptist churches choose to cooperate, this may encompass six theological seminaries, dozens of colleges and universities, and even private Christian schools and homeschooling networks.

5. False, True, True, False, True, True.

Article XIII: Stewardship

1. *Ownership* is the act, state, or right of possessing something. *Stewardship* is the management of resources belonging to someone else, as well as accountability to the owner.

2. The very idea of stewardship may be traced to the garden of Eden, where God commands Adam and Eve, "Be fruitful, multiply, fill the earth, and subdue it" (Gen. 1:28).

3. Parable of the talents (Matt. 25:14-30) – true disciples are rewarded for their faithfulness, while false professors of the faith expose their unbelief through infidelity; parable of the rich fool (Luke 12:16-21) – there are dire consequences for storing up treasures for oneself; parable of the dishonest manager (Luke 16:1-13) – an abuse of stewardship reveals that one is not truly a Christian.

4. The *Levitical tithe* supported those who offered daily sacrifices on behalf of the people. The *festival tithe* required Israelites to bring food for themselves and the Levites on special feast days. The *welfare tithe*, offered every third year, went for support of the Levite, foreigner, orphan, and widow. In addition, there were *freewill offerings*. There is some question as to whether these requirements under the Mosaic Law carry forward to the church today. If they do, few practice them. Statistically, only a small percentage of Christians

give ten percent of their gross income to the local church, and a 22 percent tither is rare.

5. See the correct answers below:

	Christians should give ...
Luke 6:38; 2 Corinthians 9:6	Liberally
Luke 21:1-4; 2 Corinthians 8:2	Sacrificially
1 Corinthians 16:1	Locally
1 Corinthians 16:2	Consistently; proportionately
2 Corinthians 9:7	Cheerfully

Article XIV: Cooperation

1. Southern Baptists realize the limitations of their churches' resources and understand that joining hands with other like-minded churches enables them to accomplish more together than they ever could alone.

2. In Acts 15 and Galatians 2, representatives of the churches in Antioch and Jerusalem met voluntarily to discuss the Judaizer controversy. They respected each other's autonomy while reaching an agreement that preserved both unity in fellowship and the doctrinal conviction of salvation by grace alone, through faith alone, in Christ alone. In 1 Corinthians 16:1 and 2 Corinthians 8-9, Paul pleads with the churches of Macedonia and Greece to gather funds for the relief of suffering Jewish Christians in Jerusalem.

3. True, True, False, True, False, True.

4. Associations – networks of churches in a geographical region such as a county or a group of neighboring counties; state conventions – networks of churches across a state or, in some cases, a region such as the northwest United States; Southern Baptist Convention – a network of roughly 47,000 independent churches that work together for the purpose of proclaiming the gospel of Jesus Christ to all people everywhere.

5. The Cooperative Program is the funding process Southern Baptists have used since 1925 to support missions at the state, national, and international levels. Through CP, the ministry reach of each local church extends around the world as 47,000 cooperating Southern Baptist churches join hands to fulfill the Great Commission.

Article XV: The Christian and the Social Order

1. False, True, True, True, False, False.

2. We live in a sinful and fallen world, a world that is "groaning" beneath the weight of sin, waiting for the return of Jesus to set things right. As Christians, who share this fallen world with unbelievers and experience the same consequences of suffering, pain, and death, we should seek to live peaceably with all people. This includes being involved in the public affairs of our community, state, and nation.

3. Children's Homes – foster care; adoption; orphan care; rescue from human trafficking; pregnancy resource centers; Baptist Homes – senior adult care; hospice care; Hospitals / Clinics – healthcare; wellness; Relief Networks – disaster relief; feeding programs; refugee assistance.

4. As Christians, we should grasp the reality that we live in a fallen world. Despite our best efforts, we are unable to eradicate sin from society, or even completely from our own lives. At the same time, we should see that when Jesus returns, he is going to purge the world of sin

and its stain and create new heavens and a new earth. Even we will be perfected – that is, fully conformed to the image of Christ. The so-called "previous things" – death, grief, crying, and pain – are banished from the new heavens and new earth.

5. One example is disaster relief, in which Missouri Baptist Disaster Relief and the Southern Baptist Convention's SEND Relief work closely with the Red Cross and various governmental agencies to provide food, shelter, clothing, and other services to survivors of natural and manmade disasters.

Article XVI: Peace and War

1. Jesus is not prohibiting Christians from engaging in warfare under all circumstances. He even engages in violent measures at times. For example, he overturns the money-changers' tables at the temple and drives away those who sell sacrificial animals at inflated prices. And when he returns to earth one day, he wears a bloody robe and strikes the nations with the sword of his mouth. The point of Matthew 5:9 ("Blessed are the peacemakers") seems to be that we cannot truly live at peace with our neighbors until "the God of peace" resides in our hearts (Rom. 15:33).

2. True, False, False, True, True, True.

3. Before his betrayal and arrest, Jesus tells his followers to carry swords for self-defense, likely to ensure he is not taken before the appointed time (Luke 22:36-38). But a short time later, he rebukes Peter for taking the offense with a sword and cutting off the ear of the high priest's servant (Luke 22:49-51). Jesus' time had come to surrender to the necessity of the cross, and violence wielded in opposition to Christ's passion was rebellion against his Father's will.

4. The correct answers are: (a), (c), and (d).

5. Matthew 24:6 – wars and rumors of wars will characterize the present

age until Christ returns; Romans 12:18 – Christians should strive to live at peace with everyone; Ephesians 6:12 – the Christian's battle is not against flesh and blood but against "evil, spiritual forces in the heavens;" Revelation 19:11-21 – Jesus returns wearing a blood-stained robe, destroying his enemies with the sword from his mouth.

Article XVII: Religious Liberty

1. Religious liberty means equality before the law for Christians and non-Christians alike. It means the freedom to worship God, or not to worship God. Religious liberty is neither a license to live recklessly, nor is it merely toleration of those who believe differently. Religious liberty does not stand on political platforms or hang from legal pillars. While civil authorities may proclaim religious tolerance, only God may grant religious freedom.

2. Matthew 22:21 – we should pay our taxes; Acts 5:29 – when the commands of any authority conflict with the clear teachings of Scripture, we must obey God rather than people; Romans 13:1-7 – we should submit to those in authority over us; 1 Timothy 2:1-2 – we should pray for our leaders; 1 Peter 2:13-17 – we should honor those in authority over us – even corrupt rulers.

3. False, True, True, False, True, True.

4. It's biblically warranted to disobey those in authority over us when those authorities command us to do something God forbids, or when they forbid us from doing something God commands.

5. In Romans 13:1-8, Paul says God establishes the authorities over us; those who resist these authorities are opposing God; the authorities exist to promote good and to punish evil; and Christians are to pay taxes, tolls, respect, and honor to those in authority over us. In a similar manner, Peter writes that we should submit to every authority as we honor the God-ordained function of rulers to promote good and punish evil; that our good conduct silences the ignorance of foolish people who oppose

legitimate authority and question Christians' submission to that authority; that we are to submit freely, not using our freedom as a cover-up for evil; and that we should honor everyone, love our brothers and sisters in Christ, fear God, and even honor the emperor (who, in Peter's day, was hostile to Christianity).

Article XVIII: The Family

1. The consistent standard of Scripture is that marriage is the uniting of one man and one woman in covenant commitment for a lifetime. The gift of sexual intimacy is for pleasure and procreation within the confines of monogamous marriage, requiring unselfishness and purity.

2. In Scripture, Jesus often is depicted as the bridegroom, with the church as his bride. Further, husbands are commanded to love their wives as Christ loved the church and gave himself for her. Wives are equal partners in marriage, with the God-given responsibility to respect their husbands and serve as their helpers in managing the household and nurturing the next generation. There is to be lasting commitment, selfless love, and intimacy in marriage, just as there is in a Christian's relationship with Christ.

3. True, True, False, False, True, False.

4. Genesis 1:26-27 – God created men and women in his image; that means the gifts of marriage, family, and gender are established for our good; Genesis 2:18-25 – marriage is the first institution God ordains, and he does so before the Fall; Romans 8:14-17 – Yahweh is a relational God, and he made us to thrive in relationships as well; he even adopts followers of Jesus as his sons and daughters; Hebrews 13:4 – the gift of sexual intimacy is for pleasure and procreation within the confines of monogamous marriage, requiring unselfishness and purity; Revelation 19:7 – marriage should be highly prized, for it is given to us as a metaphor for the relationship between Christ and his church; the Lord Jesus is depicted as the bridegroom, and his church is the bride.

5. Gender confusion is a conflict between a person's physical gender and the gender with which he or she identifies. Followers of Jesus are to treat those who struggle with gender confusion with compassion and understanding, knowing that we, too, are subject to frailties of our own. At the same time, we should help our friends rediscover God's gift of gender, sharing a biblical view of what it means to be men and women created in the image of God.

Notes

Introduction: What is *The Baptist Faith & Message*?

1. "Resolution No. 4: On Knowing and Teaching the Baptist Faith and Message 2000," *Tuesday Morning Business Update*, MBC Annual Meeting, Oct. 26, 2021.

2. Herschel H. Hobbs, *The Baptist Faith and Message* (Nashville, TN: Convention Press, 1971), 13, 16.

3. *The Baptist Faith & Message: A Statement Adopted by the Southern Baptist Convention, June 14, 2000* (Nashville, TN: Lifeway Press, 2000; reprinted 2021), 3-4.

4. For an overview of the fundamentalist-modernist controversy, see John R. Muether, "The Fundamentalist-Modernist Controversy," https://tabletalkmagazine.com/article/2020/05/the-fundamentalist-modernist-controversy/.

5. Preamble to the 1925 *Baptist Faith & Message*, https://bfm.sbc.net/comparison-chart/.

6. Preamble to the 1963 *Baptist Faith & Message*, https://bfm
.sbc.net/comparison-chart/.

7. Preamble to *The Baptist Faith & Message* 2000, https://bfm
.sbc.net/comparison-chart/.

Article I: The Scriptures

1. Article I of "Comparison Chart," https://bfm.sbc.net/comparison
-chart/.

2. Charles C. Ryrie, *Basic Theology: A Popular Systematic Guide To
Understanding Biblical Truth* (Wheaton, IL: Victor Books, 1986), 71.

3. P. D. Feinberg in *Evangelical Dictionary of Theology*, ed. Walter A.
Elwell (Grand Rapids, MI: Baker Books, 2001), n.p.

4. Chicago Statement on Biblical Inerrancy with Exposition, Article
XII, http://www.bible-researcher.com/chicago1.html.

5. Wayne Grudem, *Systematic Theology: An Introduction to Biblical
Doctrine* (Leicester, England: InterVarsity Press; Grand Rapids, MI:
Zondervan, 1994), 127.

Article II: God

1. Article II of "Comparison Chart," https://bfm.sbc.net/comparison
-chart/.

2. J. I. Packer, *Concise Theology: A Guide to Historic Christian Beliefs*
(Carol Stream, IL: Tyndale House Publishers, Inc., 1993), 42.

3. Freddy Davis, "Why Belief in the Trinity is Essential in Christianity
– Part 2: The Importance of the Doctrine of the Trinity," *Worldview
Made Practical*, Vol. 10, No. 22, June 10, 2015, 1.

4. Nabeel Qureshi, *No God But One: Allah or Jesus?* (Grand Rapids, MI: Zondervan, 2016), 65.

5. "The Trinity," *The Valley of Vision: A Collection of Puritan Prayers & Devotions*, ed. Arthur Bennett (Edinburgh, UK; Carlisle, PA: The Banner of Truth Trust, 1975), 2-3.

Article II-A: God the Father

1. Article II-A of "Comparison Chart," https://bfm.sbc.net/comparison-chart/.

Article II-B: God the Son

1. Article II-B of "Comparison Chart," https://bfm.sbc.net/comparison-chart/.

2. Bruce Ware, *The Man Christ Jesus: Theological Reflections on the Humanity of Christ* (Wheaton, IL: Crossway, 2012), 26.

Article II-C: God the Holy Spirit

1. Article II-C of "Comparison Chart," https://bfm.sbc.net/comparison-chart/.

2. "The Spirit of Jesus," *The Valley of Vision*, 58-59. [Note: the words "Instil" and "fulfilment" in the original were updated to read "Instill" and "fulfillment."]

Article III: Man

1. Article III of "Comparison Chart," https://bfm.sbc.net/comparison-chart/.

2. Charles S. Kelley Jr., Richard Land, and R. Albert Mohler Jr., *The Baptist Faith & Message*, 6-part Bible Study (Nashville, TN: LifeWay Press, 2007), 63.

Article IV: Salvation

1. Article IV of "Comparison Chart," https://bfm.sbc.net /comparison-chart/.

2. According to Alfred Edersheim, a teacher of languages and Warbutonian Lecturer at Lincoln's Inn (Oxford), there are at least 465 messianic references in the Old Testament. See John Ankerberg, John Weldon, and Walter C. Kaiser Jr., *The Case for Jesus the Messiah: Incredible Prophecies That Prove God Exists* (Chattanooga, TN: The John Ankerberg Evangelistic Association, 1989), 12.

Article IV-A: Regeneration

1. Article IV-A of "Comparison Chart," https://bfm.sbc.net /comparison-chart/.

2. Rob Phillips, *What Every Christian Should Know About Salvation: Twelve Bible Terms That Describe God's Work of Redemption* (Jefferson City, MO: High Street Press, 2018), 85-91.

3. Kenneth Keathley, *Salvation and Sovereignty: A Molinist Approach* (Nashville, TN: B&H Publishing Group, 2010), 101.

Article IV-B: Justification

1. Article IV-B of "Comparison Chart," https://bfm.sbc.net /comparison-chart/.

Article IV-C: Sanctification

1. Article IV-C of "Comparison Chart," https://bfm.sbc.net /comparison-chart/. Also, for more on Southern Baptists' denial of the false doctrine of "sinless perfection," see Hobbs, 61-62.

2. Millard J. Erickson, *Christian Theology*, Third Edition (Grand Rapids, MI: Baker Academic, 2013), 897.

3. John M. Frame, *Systematic Theology: An Introduction to Christian Belief* (Phillipsburg, NJ: P&R Publishing Company, 2013), 986.

Article IV-D: Glorification

1. Article IV-D of "Comparison Chart," https://bfm.sbc.net /comparison-chart/.

2. Grudem, 828.

3. William D. Mounce, *Mounce's Complete Expository Dictionary of Old & New Testament Words* (Grand Rapids, MI: Zondervan, 2006), 290.

Article IV-D: Our Glorified Bodies

1. Article IV-D of "Comparison Chart," https://bfm.sbc.net /comparison-chart/.

2. Kenneth E. Bailey, *Paul Through Mediterranean Eyes: Cultural Studies in 1 Corinthians* (Downers Grove, IL: IVP Academic, 2011), 467.

Article V: God's Purpose of Grace

1. Article V of "Comparison Chart," https://bfm.sbc.net
/comparison-chart/.

2. Keathley, 5.

3. For a more detailed discussion of foreknowledge, election, and predestination, see Phillips, *What Every Christian Should Know About Salvation*, 3-48.

4. "Election," *The Valley of Vision*, 88.

Article VI: The Church

1. Article VI of "Comparison Chart," https://bfm.sbc.net
/comparison-chart/.

2. The Greek words corresponding to *bishop, elder,* and *pastor* are: *episkope* (bishop, overseer); *presbuteros* (elder); and *poimen* (pastor, shepherd).

Article VII: Baptism and the Lord's Supper

1. Article VII of "Comparison Chart," https://bfm.sbc.net
/comparison-chart/.

2. *Vine's Expository Dictionary of New Testament Words*, "Baptizo, B-1, verb, Strong's Number G907," https://www.blueletterbible.org/search
/dictionary/viewtopic.cfm?topic=VT0000215.

Article VIII: The Lord's Day

1. Article VIII of "Comparison Chart," https://bfm.sbc.net /comparison-chart/.

2. David Schrock, "7 Things You Should Know About the Lord's Day," https://www.thegospelcoalition.org/reviews/a-brief-history-of-sunday/.

3. Justo L. Gonzalez, *A Brief History of Sunday: From the New Testament to the New Creation* (Grand Rapids, MI: William B. Eerdmans Publishing Company, 2017), 29.

4. Gonzalez, 39, 43.

5. Kelley, Land, and Mohler, 103.

6. "The Lord's Day," *The Valley of Vision*, 354-355.

Article IX: The Kingdom

1. Article IX of "Comparison Chart," https://bfm.sbc.net/comparison -chart/.

2. George Eldon Ladd, *The Gospel of the Kingdom: Scriptural Studies in the Kingdom of God* (Grand Rapids, MI: William B. Eerdmans Publishing Company, 1959), 19.

3. Kelley, Land, and Mohler, 109.

Article X: Last Things

1. Article X of "Comparison Chart," https://bfm.sbc.net/comparison -chart/.

Article XI: Evangelism and Missions

1. Article XI of "Comparison Chart," https://bfm.sbc.net/comparison -chart/.

2. Jessica Brodie, "What Is Evangelism? Should We All Be Evangelists?", https://www.christianity.com/wiki/christian-terms/what -is-evangelism.html, July 8, 2020.

3. Hobbs, 108.

4. Kelley, Land, and Mohler, 123.

5. Hobbs, 109.

6. "The Servant in Battle," *The Valley of Vision*, 328-329.

Article XII: Education

1. Article XII of "Comparison Chart," https://bfm.sbc.net/comparison -chart/.

2. Kelley, Land, and Mohler, 133.

Article XIII: Stewardship

1. Article XIII of "Comparison Chart," https://bfm.sbc.net/comparison -chart/.

2. Hobbs, 118.

3. Hobbs, 121.

Article XIV: Cooperation

1. Article XIV of "Comparison Chart," https://bfm.sbc.net/comparison-chart/.

2. Hobbs, 124.

3. *Fast Facts*, https://www.sbc.net/about/what-we-do/fast-facts/.

Article XV: The Christian and the Social Order

1. Article XV of "Comparison Chart," https://bfm.sbc.net/comparison-chart/.

2. Kelley, Land, and Mohler, 149.

3. Hobbs, 129.

4. Kelley, Land, and Mohler, 153.

5. M. E. Dodd, quoted by Emir and Ergun Caner in *The Sacred Trust: Sketches of the Southern Baptist Presidents* (Nashville, TN: Broadman & Holman Publishers, 2003), 77-78.

Article XVI: Peace and War

1. Article XVI of "Comparison Chart," https://bfm.sbc.net/comparison-chart/.

2. Chris Hedges, "What Every Person Should Know About War," *New York Times*, July 6, 2003, https://www.nytimes.com/2003/07/06/books/chapters/what-every-person-should-know-about-war.html.

3. *Ibid.*

4. "War and Peace," https://www.bbc.co.uk/bitesize/guides/zbygjxs /revision/5.

5. *Ibid.*; also Kelley, Land, and Mohler, 157.

Article XVII: Religious Liberty

1. Article XVII of "Comparison Chart," https://bfm.sbc.net /comparison-chart/.

2. Hobbs, 141.

3. *James P. Boyce: Treasures from the Baptist Heritage,* Timothy and Denise George, eds., (Nashville, TN: Broadman & Holman Publishers, 1996), 241-242.

4. Hobbs, 143.

Article XVIII: The Family

1. Article XVIII of "Comparison Chart," https://bfm.sbc.net /comparison-chart/.

2. Kelley, Land, and Mohler, 170.

3. *The Baptist Faith & Message* 2000, Article XVIII.

4. Kelley, Land, and Mohler, 168.

5. Jonathan T. Pennington, "The Cultural Context," Jewish Life in the Days of Jesus, *Tabletalk,* Feb. 2022, Vol. 46, No. 2, 21.

6. Kelley, Land, and Mohler, 169.

Additional Resources

Order additional materials from
High Street Press

Featured Item

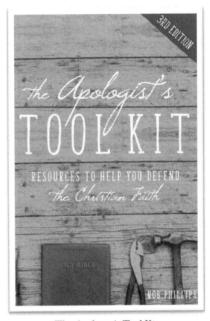

The Apologist's Tool Kit:
Resources to Help You
Defend the Christian Faith

The apostle Peter urges Christians to "always be ready to give a defense to anyone who asks you for a reason for the hope that is in you," and to do so "with gentleness and respect" (1 Pet. 3:15-16).

The Apologist's Tool Kit equips you to defend the Christian faith in just this way. This easy-to-read reference addresses some of the most commonly challenged Christian doctrines, from the existence of God to the authority of Scripture. Each chapter concludes with probing questions, talking points, and references for further reading, making this a handy resource for personal or group study.

Print and Kindle editions are available from Amazon. Print editions also are available from other booksellers. For discounted bulk orders, contact cdowell@mobaptist.org.

Other Titles

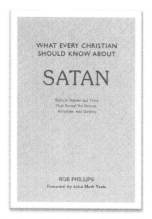

What Every Christian Should Know About Satan: Biblical Names and Titles That Reveal His Nature, Activities, And Destiny

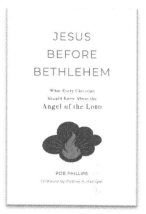

Jesus Before Bethlehem: What Every Christian Should Know About the Angel of the LORD

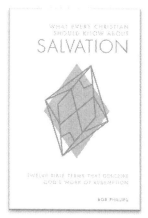

What Every Christian Should Know About Salvation: Twelve Bible Terms That Describe God's Work of Redemption

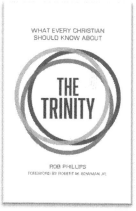

What Every Christian Should Know About the Trinity: How the Bible Reveals One God in Three Persons

Order these books and more through the retailers listed at our website: highstreet.press/titles.

The Last Apologist: A Commentary on Jude
for Defenders of the Christian Faith

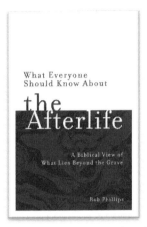

What Everyone Should Know About the
Afterlife: A Biblical View of What Lies
Beyond the Grave

What Every Christian Should Know About
Islam: A Primer on the Muslim Faith from
a Biblical Worldview

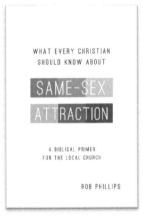

What Every Christian Should Know About
Same-Sex Attraction: A Biblical Primer
for the Local Church

Audio-book editions of *Jesus Before Bethlehem* and *What Everyone Should Know About the Afterlife* are available at Audible.com. An audio-book version of *What Every Christian Should Know About Satan* is available Fall 2022 at Audible.com.

Made in the USA
Middletown, DE
16 February 2023